THE GIFT OF
LISTENING

THE GIFT OF
LISTENING

Robert Brizee

Chalice Press
St. Louis, Missouri

All scripture quotations, unless otherwise indicated, are from the *New Revised Standard Version Bible*, copyright 1989, Division of Christian Education of the National Council of the Churches of Christ in the USA. Used by permission.

Cover Art: Glenn Myers

Art Director: Michael Dominguez

11/9⁴

Library of Congress Cataloging-in-Publication Data

Brizee. Robert.
  The gift of listening / by Robert Brizee.
ISBN 0-8272-1237-2
1. Listening—Religious aspects—Christianity.   I. Title.
BV4647.L56B75 1993   242   92-32061

Printed in the United States of America

Bookstore

Contents

Acknowledgments

While this book is a creation of my own imagination, I was deeply influenced by others. I wish to acknowledge them and express my deep gratitude.

Dr. David Ray Griffin suggested that I write about listening. My pastor, Dr. Mary Ann Swenson, and my friend, Connie Nelson, R.N., offered pivotal proposals that made the story I have created more genuine. My wife, Adrienne Brizee, M.S., has thought out ideas with me, co-led seminars on listening, encouraged me in difficult moments, and carried extra household burdens as I processed words.

I am particularly grateful to two groups of people who helped to make the listening dialogues throughout the book more realistic. They marked up, red-lined, and edited the words I had written. The first group was made up of those who participated in our church family life seminar on the gift of listening in the winter quarter of 1992.

The second was the staff of the First United Methodist Church of Wenatchee, Washington, who carefully reviewed the dialogues in chapter six, "Imagining a Listening Church." I considered them eminently qualified to improve my presentations because of their daily involvement in a local congregation. I thank Dr. Mary Ann Swenson, the Rev. Ed Branham, Ms. Mary Gates, Ms. Jackie Griffiths, Ms. Melissa McCormick, and Mr. Al Skelton. Their suggestions were invaluable.

My sincere gratitude goes to Dr. David Polk, my former classmate, colleague in process and faith endeavors, and now my editor. I am grateful that he and his editorial staff saw an important message in something that I have held dear to my heart for years.

Introduction

Listening is a gift. My deeply held conviction is that to listen to another is to offer that person a gift. I affirm that all of us yearn for this gift, and nearly all of us can offer it. Every person is called to be a listener. It is healing to be heard and accepted just as we are. My own experience of thirty-five years in a profession of listening convinces me of the truth of that healing.

The gift is even more deeply enhanced for me when I know that God is present and luring within the person to whom I listen. We listen to heal, but also we listen to increase another's awareness of the ever-present and gracious whispering of God. To live increasingly in the awareness of a deeply moving divine process is genuine healing. I, therefore, offer a theology of listening and affirm that the church has a unique ministry of listening.

Three perspectives inform this proposed theology of listening: the biblical research on Abba, the theological vision of process relational theology, and the psychological discipline of listening. They can be summarized briefly: God is Abba for Jesus, God is an ever-present Caring Friend, and listening is a healing process.

I made a deliberate choice to illustrate listening in story form. I hope that this will allow you, the reader, to identify the need to be heard with a particular family living in a particular location. I found this approach required more struggle and creativity on my part, but ultimately I experienced it as more rewarding. My wish is that you would feel with this family such that they become a part of your "circle of friends."

I am painfully aware that my imaginary family and church will not sound "real"! I know my imaginary dialogues will sound strange, perhaps too optimistic. We do not talk the way that I have imagined. Rather, often we talk sharply and hurtfully in our intimate relationships. I am offering what might be a new possibility. I hope that in time, perhaps in several generations or a century, we may listen the way that I imagine it here.

I chose also to illustrate listening in a group, in addition to the more common situation of person to person. One listening to several and several listening to one are offered as a potential design for the church.

Chapter one describes the deep yearning to be heard, presents the three undergirding perspectives, and introduces the family and their setting. Chapters two through five propose four listening styles, illustrating them by showing how listening assists this family toward a solution to a perplexing problem. Chapter six creates an imaginary church, showing how listening may be a valued skill in all phases of congregational life.

My intention is to encourage the church to include the ministry of listening as an important addition to its more traditional missions.

A prelude to this book may be stated simply as follows:

To listen to another person is to offer a gift.

To listen with caring to another person is to offer a gift of awareness.

To listen with acceptance to all facets of another person is to offer a gift of healing.

To listen with patience for new ways to see the past events of another person is to offer a gift of freedom.

To listen with reverence for new becomings emerging within another person is to offer a gift of grace.

1

A Longing to Be Heard

*He said, "Abba, Father, for you all
things are possible; remove this cup
from me; yet, not what I want, but
what you want."*
Mark 14:36

Deep within us is a longing to be
heard. I know this as surely as I know my own name.
Everyone needs to be heard and nearly everyone can
listen. On these two deeply held convictions rest all that I
will say here.

It seems obvious that when in crisis, we need to be
heard. Whether grieving the untimely death of a loved
one, waiting for an important letter, reeling from a job
loss, suffering from failing an important examination, or
recoiling from some dreaded diagnosis, we certainly need
to pour out our feelings to one who cares.

Being heard is just as important when we stand at
difficult crossroads. Struggling with what to do after
graduation, wondering whether to marry at this time,
puzzling over a job offer, weighing the benefits of moving,
or deciding if this is the house to buy all cry out for
someone to listen.

It is less obvious that we need to talk regularly about our everyday events. Making sense out of the happenings of our day is the basic and simple need. We are continually creating meaning out of our stream of experience: our feelings, our fleeting thoughts, our insights, our night dreams, and our daydreams. These, though appearing less urgent, speak of the deep longing to be heard. Knowing this to be true compels me to claim that everyone needs to be heard.

Even young children are fitting new experiences into their own visions of the world and how the world works.[1] For them it is important to integrate finding a dead bird on the school playground or being dealt with unfairly in a classroom with their present worldview. They need desperately to be heard, if for no other reason than that they may otherwise draw severe, false, or harmful conclusions about life and themselves.

I know of the terrible results that occur when this longing to be heard is not satisfied. The long-term effects are usually feelings of self-doubt and aloneness.

If I speak and am rebuffed, discounted, or told that I am wrong, self-doubt occurs. My inner talk may be like this: *I thought that I knew what I felt, but now that someone who knows more than I do says that I couldn't possibly feel that way, I really must be wrong. I guess that I don't know me after all. I must not be able to think straight.* In this process, that which is most precious to us all, our own trust in our own experiences, is taken away.

In a similar vein, if I never had anyone with whom to share, I am likely to begin talking to myself in this way: *I'm feeling this, but I never hear anyone else feeling that way. There must be something really wrong with me if I have this feeling. I sure don't want to tell anyone else about this or they'll laugh at me or not want to be around me. I guess I must be pretty strange.* In this process, the sense of aloneness grows stronger and stronger, the feeling of strangeness greater and greater.

While my examples are of extremes, I am convinced that to some degree all of us go through similar processes of self-talk when our deep longing to be heard is not fulfilled. In certain ways our present society adds to the problem. Our days are filled with distractions that keep us from both knowing our own longing and listening to those around us: the music is so loud, the television so alluring, the pace so fast, and the tasks so many. I sense the remarkable difference when I contrast our present surroundings with the many hours of near quietness I experienced as a youth riding a horse-drawn hay rake in the alfalfa fields of a large cattle ranch.

I know the longing to be heard, both from within my own being and through the crying out I have heard. I know the agony when this longing is ignored. But more than that I know the deep joy that arises when one speaks and is heard by another. When I know that what I say is important to another, I am healed. Those who offer such understanding and caring engage in healing.

I am even more convinced that those of us who are within the community of the church have a potential for listening that is unsurpassed. Sharing this conviction will be a central theme in all that follows. All persons long to be heard, nearly all may hear. We in the church have a special reason and call to listen.

Let us now turn to a special vision of God that I believe empowers us to listen. First, I wish to describe how this vision was gifted to us by Jesus. This, in turn, will allow me to illustrate how we may learn to listen through the story of a particular family living in a particular place.

What does God have to do with our listening to one another? At first glance the answer could easily be: nothing! It may even sound like a strange question. At second glance one might answer that it is a caring thing to do and God surely desires that we be caring, so God will smile upon our endeavor. In a similar vein, listening often seems to help the other person and God would encourage our helping others. Indeed, listening is healing to another and God certainly calls us to engage in healing.

If we grant those statements to be true, I affirm that God has even more to do with listening. I am proposing that it is because of who God is that we engage in listening to others. Our reason for listening goes directly to our understanding of God. Allow me to expand this belief by the following affirmations: God is an Intimate Friend who is with us in every moment. God is influencing, persuading, and calling us in each of those moments. By listening to others we help them to become increasingly aware of God's creative presence within them. They come to know more fully how God is participating in their lives. We are, then, listening for God's presence in the life of another.

Having declared it in a brief form, I wish to share how I came to this conviction. There is a clear trail by which I reached that destination. The primary path that I took was the experience of Jesus as he addressed God as "Dada." Before Jesus no one used this manner of speaking to God. A unique event is before us.

Let us begin our journey by consulting the Bible. In doing so I will point to a few particular events rather than cite multiple examples of people listening to people, followed by the call to go and do likewise. The opposite is found: proclaim! The central emphasis is to preach and witness. If listening is encouraged at all, it is to hear that which is being proclaimed. The Bible is clearly not a manual on listening. Nevertheless, a call to listen is present if we will be patient and explore the longer trail to hear it. Obviously, I believe the beautiful destination is worth the trip. Having opened the scriptures, now let us trace the history of how God has been both understood and addressed.

For this history, I am indebted to the scholarly work of Joachim Jeremias.[2] According to Jeremias, Jesus was not the first to use the word *Father* for God. His Hebrew forebears had both thought of God and addressed God in this form, but they used it only fifteen times in the entire Hebrew Bible. Moreover, when they used it they had a clear picture of whom they addressed: the Father was

first and foremost the Creator of the universe and of a
people.

The Father as Creator was also Lord, whose will
always prevailed and who was honored by obedience.
God was the adoptive Father to this unique people, Israel, not their biological Father. God chose, elected, saved,
and delivered this band of people, forming them into a
community. In this sense of adoption, God differed from
the gods of other cultures in the Middle East.

Interwoven with the Creator, Lord, adoptive parent
image was the tender, forgiving one. While the children
were continually disobedient to God, repeatedly God would
be merciful and forgive their waywardness.

> With weeping they shall come,
>   and with consolations I will lead them back,
> I will let them walk by brooks of water,
>   in a straight path in which they shall not
>   stumble;
> for I have become a father to Israel,
>   and Ephraim is my firstborn.
>   Jeremiah 31:9

> Is Ephraim my dear son?
>   Is he the child I delight in?...
> Therefore I am deeply moved for him;
>   I will surely have mercy on him,
>   says the LORD.
>   Jeremiah 31:20

To this great mercy offered, the community responded:
"Thou art our Father!"[3] God was, however, Father to the
entire community, Ephraim. God was the individual's
Father only because that person was a member of the
covenant community of Israel. This differs from God as
my personal Father.

In the prayer life of Judaism in the time of Jesus, two
instances addressing God as Father have been discovered, both a part of the temple liturgy:

Our Father, our King,
for the sake of our fathers,
who trusted upon thee
and whom thou taughtest the statutes of life—
have mercy upon us and teach us.

Our Father, our King,
we have no other king but thee;
our Father, our King,
for thine own sake have mercy upon us.[4]

Once again, these are instances of the community addressing God. It is *our Father*. Moreover, the title is intimately bound to another powerful image, "King." There have, however, been no discoveries yet of a personal prayer beginning with *Father* in that era. Equally important, the Psalms, the corporate worship of the people, never give voice to the title *Father*.

In the midst of this form of worship, a dramatically new voice spoke. Jesus began every prayer with *Father*. The contrast is clear. That which was seldom if ever used suddenly began to be used always. Not only the use of the word but the one to whom it referred was radically different. Jesus reached into the realm of family life rather than temple worship to find the language of prayer. He chose the only word available in that era to describe "dada." To say the least, this action was considered radical, probably more likely disrespectful and blasphemous.

Jesus did not choose the word *abhi*, which had been used in temple worship, usually in the phrase, "Our Father, who art in heaven." I expect it would have been more familiar and accepted by those of his day. He chose *abba*, the name first spoken by the infant in calling to a parent. The two words uttered were *imma* and *abba*, obviously *mama* and *dada*. The Talmud says: "When a child experiences the taste of wheat it learns to say 'abba' and 'imma.'"[5] The translation would be: when a child is weaned these are the first sounds that he or she makes. To this realm of childhood Jesus turned to express his relationship with God.

I am most impressed that Jesus spoke in the same simple, emotional, elementary language as a small child crying out to a parent. It is revealing of the relationship between Jesus and God. Yet, lest we think of it as only a childlike utterance, in the days of Jesus adults addressed their parents using this same word. Thus, it is not limited to the language of childhood but rather encompasses the intimate language of the family.

Jesus spoke always of the Father and always addressed the Father as "abba," but today in our scripture we read it as the Greek *pater*, with one known exception. Can we trust that the Greek really refers back to this particular Aramaic word? Could it not have been some other word translated to Father? Jeremias answers, "No." There were no other words for father in that culture in that era.[6]

The one possibility, already mentioned, *abhi*, was obsolete by this time in Palestinian Judaism, as was its meaning of "my lord."[7] Scholarship tells us that we can trust that when we read *Father* in our English translations of the Bible, the Greek underlying this is *pater* and the Aramaic underlying that is *abba*.

It is compelling to me that in three New Testament passages, the original Aramaic is left intact, although the text itself was penned in Greek. The first is found in a Gospel, the remaining two in letters of Paul:

He said, "Abba, Father, for you all things are possible; remove this cup from me; yet, not what I want, but what you want."

Mark 14:36;
parallels: Matthew 26:39; Luke 22:42

And because you are children, God has sent the Spirit of his Son into our hearts, crying, "Abba! Father!"

Galatians 4:6

> When we cry, "Abba! Father!" it is that very Spirit bearing witness with our spirit that we are children of God.
>
> Romans 8:15–16

In every instance but one, when Jesus prays the one addressed is Father. (Mark 14:36; Matthew 6:9; Luke 10:21; Luke 23:34, 46; John 11:41, 42) The one exception is the agonizing prayer on the cross, when it is widely accepted that Jesus was praying a psalm rather than offering a personal prayer (Mark 15:34): "My God, my God, why have you forsaken me?"(Psalm 22:1).

Confirming evidence of the relationship of Jesus with God as "Abba! Father!" comes from the number of times that he uses this title when speaking about God. As the Gospel tradition grows from Mark through Matthew and Luke to John, the use of *Father* increases as well. The early church surely affirmed this title. That Paul would retain the original Aramaic word in his early letters forms another strand of evidence apart from the Gospel tradition. There seems little doubt: Jesus prayed to God and talked about God as *papa*.

Jesus spoke to his disciples about *your Father* in contrast to his personal use of *my Father*. He did not speak to the crowds in either manner. This intimate family language was reserved for the followers.

Jesus' intimacy and closeness with God is amazing, yet no more so than his offering this familiarity to his disciples. The wondrous relationship that he experienced as "abba," he offered to them.

> "Lord, teach us to pray, as John taught his disciples." He said to them, "When you pray, say: 'Father, hallowed be your name....'"
>
> Luke 11:1–2

Jeremias concluded his research by saying, "There is as yet no evidence in the literature of ancient Palestinian Judaism that 'my Father' is used as a personal address to God."[8] Yet this is exactly how Jesus always addressed

God. His choice of the title *abba*, taken from intimate family life, to describe a religious experience is without comparison.

That a word foreign to the text is still retained is a credit to its importance. Such value was accorded *abba*. Texts recorded the unique fashion in which Jesus addressed God and the invitation to followers to enter this new and remarkable relationship.

We have before us a proposal from scripture: Jesus experienced a radically new relationship and was compelled to find a new word to capture the wondrous qualities of that relationship. An intimate family word was chosen. For me, this relationship forms the basis for listening. When we listen to another, a relationship between God and that person is present, often hovering in the distant background of awareness, but present. We listen to enhance that relationship.

Before drawing other implications for listening, I wish to follow several other shorter trails. I wonder what happened to the freshness, excitement, and astonishment of this new vision that Jesus brought to the world. Where did we lose it?

I have a sense that other facets of Jesus came to be more important. The more legal aspects may have appealed to the church as it became a powerful institution aligned with the Roman Empire. The Lord's Prayer may have taken its place in worship as one more ritual rather than as one that required the utmost courage to utter. Perhaps we have never fully grasped that *Father* had such a radical meaning for our lives. If that be so, then it is still awaiting our discovery.

Another brief trail is to wonder why Jesus chose *abba* rather than *imma*. Most of the qualities that attach to the title speak more of mother than father. I know of no clear-cut answers, but propose that it would have been highly unlikely. Sadly, women were not powerful religious images in that culture. If one were having religious experiences it would be natural to assume them to be masculine rather than feminine.

I wonder, too, if the shift to addressing God as a family member were already so radical that an even greater shift to the female family member might have led people, even disciples, to consider Jesus utterly demented. Regardless of which theory may be most accurate, it is my deep conviction that God portrays most fully those qualities that are truly *abba-imma*. Consequently, in my reflections here, I will be speaking not simply of the male *abba* image, but of the comprehensive *abba-imma* experience. It is my belief that this choice will not be a distortion of the new relationship that Jesus experienced with God.

Another important trail is that of sharing how the experiences of Jesus weave with a Christian theology in which I am grounded. I am especially pleased that the *abba-imma* experiences and this theology confirm and strengthen one another, even though they emerge from somewhat different sources.

Process relational theology began developing in the second quarter of the twentieth century, with the thought of Alfred North Whitehead, who had already made significant contributions in the fields of mathematics and philosophy.[9] Coming to the United States from Britain in his later years, he focused attention on cosmology, the theory that attempts to explain everything. Such universal scholars are rare in our day of specialization within narrow disciplines.

Whitehead began with the notion of experience as that which can ultimately explain everything from the atomic to the human. Indeed, he chose human experience as the model by which to view all other types of experience. His next novel idea was to divide human experience into units rather than consider it to be an everflowing stream. These units were called *occasions*, which could now be understood as having a beginning, later phases, and a conclusion.

In Whitehead's vision, God begins each occasion by offering a possibility for that particular event. No mere afterthought, God is central to every event of humans, animals, plants, cells, molecules, and atoms. God is actively and intimately involved in every happening in every part of the universe, calling the particular person or entity toward something better. Direction is continually offered by God in the form of persuasion.

In this cosmology, which was later integrated into a Christian theology, God is near, intimate, involved, caring, and guiding. A sharp contrast exists with any theology that pictures God as being up there showing little concern for our daily lives, as having started it all but having been uninvolved since then, or as exerting complete control over what happens in the world.

God is, rather, so intimate as to know our every feeling and thought and to offer a new possibility for our next moment based on those feelings and thoughts. Even more, God caringly feels what we feel, the ultimate empathy. In every proposal that God offers to us, there is the call toward increased love, harmony, complexity, intensity, and beauty. The call comes for us and for all creation.

My main point in summarizing this theology is to suggest that it dovetails well with the experiences of Jesus. Of course it should, since Whitehead was both aware of and indebted to the Galilean. Whether coming from the stream of *abba-imma* or the stream of cosmology, there is a confluence that swells forth with John Wesley's words, "Best of all, God is with us."

Jesus knows of God's presence through intimate personal experience and uses the language of family, while Whitehead affirms God's presence through the use of the keenly honed intellect of a skilled mathematician, philosopher, and cosmologist. Will, emotion, and commitment are confirmed by thought and reason.

So, whether I start with biblical or theological proposals, I affirm that *there is within each of us a creative process in which God is at the center*. Words usually fail when I try to describe how God is present. Perhaps the best that can be done is to approximate: Mysterious Friend, Caring One, Graceful One, Loving Presence.

Whether soaring the lofty heights of theology or walking the paths of Galilee, there is evidence offered of a caring presence ever with us offering loving guidance toward ever-increasing gracefulness. Here is the basis of a theology of listening. We listen for God's presence.

We may now return to my original question: What does God have to do with listening? I answer: much! It does make a world of difference when I assume that in listening I am entering a continuing relationship between the person and God. Such a vision makes both the goal and the style of listening unique.

We are now at the heart of the issue, the assumptions we make about the one to whom we listen. Which convictions we hold will make crucial differences in our listening. We do not hear as though we are blank pages; we do have some idea of that for which we listen.

Let us assume that I am convinced that life is composed of stimuli and responses. Persons are defined as ones who react. Their uniqueness is how they react. Persons are clusters of responses. I listen to persons, then, with this understanding. The bond between a particular stimulus and a response becomes visible, such as when one's plans go awry, one always becomes angry. The stimulus of disruption is associated with the response of anger.

No matter how far back in one's past we trace, the same realities are found: bonds of varying strengths between stimuli and responses. The strength of different bonds and that which reinforces and extinguishes those bonds become the focus of listening. The primary mystery is the occasionally unusual response. Usually a person's future is highly predictable through knowing the past.

Both past and present are composed of responses made to stimuli. There is no *abba-imma* present. There is no reason to listen for such a relationship. The question is simply which stimuli have become associated with which responses.

Let us suppose, however, that I know persons to be composed of biological urges and the pressure to restrain those urges. The drive for unlimited pleasure is met by the rules of society. As a listener I will focus upon a person's aggressive and sexual feelings and the ensuing struggles to discover acceptable ways to both control and express them.

The prime reality is the body; personality emerges from it. The bubbling biological caldron becomes the primary force in the life of the person. Finding the balance between bodily urges and social customs looms as the primary task. Here the listener would focus also.

In contrast to both of these assumptions, let us now assume that I see the person as a battleground between Satan and God. On one side is the desire to obey the will of the Lord, while on the other is the lure of the temptation of Satan. As a listener I will be attentive to the two pulls: the call and the temptation.

Whatever the person said, I would be hearing it in the context of this cosmic struggle occurring within this particular mortal. A power struggle for the person's allegiance is ever-present in each moment. Not stimulus-response bonds, nor biological urges, but cosmic battle is the reality.

We could continue to suppose other assumptions about reality. I could listen for "parent-child transactions," "games people play," "enlightened self-interest," "the dog-eat-dog survival of the fittest," or "we are what we eat." All hold an element of truth or they would not have been named or survived into our era. All answer the questions: What is real? What is going on here? What is happening in this person as I listen?

I am contending—nay, proclaiming—that the basic reality that Jesus gifted to us is what is occurring when we listen. Such a process is different than stimulus-response bonds, biology, or cosmic struggle.

Perhaps this may be further illustrated by a review of the number of reasons why we may choose to listen. While not necessarily inclusive, here are a variety of reasons. I may listen selectively to gain information from you for my diagnosis that will guide my treatment, the usual style of the healing professions. I may listen carefully to learn your wants so that I may know which service or item to offer to you, the skill of salespersons and consultants.

I may listen to find your vulnerable points so that I can win the argument, on the higher level a talented debater while on the lower level a hurtful aggressor. I may listen to test your understanding of some subject, a method of teachers and instructors. I may listen to learn more about something you already know and I want to know, the skill of able students.

I may listen to help you to know what you are feeling, a talent of good friends and counselors. I may listen to enhance your growth toward self-understanding, a regular endeavor of psychotherapists.

Now, I wish to contrast all of the above reasons for listening with one that is based upon *abba-imma*: *I listen to facilitate a process of awareness of God's presence and God's creative activity in another's life.*

While I have high regard for a number of the reasons for listening and count them as uniquely valuable, I advocate here for the theological style. This form of listening is truly a gift. It offers grace freely given. It clearly acknowledges that the listener is not the actor, healer, or doer, but is the facilitator of a relationship in which that real action occurs. When new awareness and direction emerge, it is to the credit of the relationship of the person with God.

The listener does not set the goals for the other; they emerge from the person. The listener does not gain directly from what the person concludes; the other celebrates the gain. There is no coercion from the listener; freedom belongs to the speaker. Again, listening is a *gift!*

Having shared a theology of listening, it is important to review a brief history of listening itself. A new day occurred for listening when Carl Rogers published his work on client-centered therapy in 1951.[10] Prior to this time most professionals followed the rich tradition of the medical model of listening long enough to form a diagnosis from which to develop a treatment plan. The professional was in control by setting both the goals and the steps to achieve them. The listening was quite selective for the purpose of detecting symptoms of a particular illness. Crucial questions were asked and the answers were listened to carefully.

Rogers turned this around. He listened to the client first. His interest was to find out what that person wanted, what was blocking the achievement of that want, and how the person might find ways to remove the block. The goal belonged to the speaker, as did the steps to get there. The listener became the one who carefully walked into the speaker's world, understanding and feeling with each step. As the speaker felt caringly understood, the process of healing began and grew. Listening was client-centered!

This new approach was highly influential in many professions: psychotherapy, counseling, personnel management, and ministry. It directly affected many World War II veterans who sought education under the G.I. Bill, for many of the Veteran's Administration counselors were trained by Rogers. From a beginning as veteran's guidance centers, many university counseling centers were formed on campuses, again with a Rogerian emphasis. Our culture had been changed.

A colleague of Rogers, Thomas Gordon, named this style of listening and offered it to the masses. *Active listening* became a central feature of both the book and program of *Parent Effectiveness Training*.[11] Thousands of persons have been trained to know when and how to listen to their children. Parents in the 1970s now had a mentor other than Dr. Spock. Rogers and Gordon have done much to popularize listening, bringing it into our living rooms and kitchens, and I personally have the highest respect for their contributions.

My indebtedness to both will be evident as this work unfolds. Nevertheless, I have not found a theology of listening in their work, nor did they intend one. I do! I firmly believe that the important concepts and techniques of their theories can be embraced and interwoven with the theology of *abba-imma* to form a comprehensive approach.

Their deep respect for the human person as one who deserves to be heard, and their basic trust in the process that may unfold between speaker and listener, can be even more healing when undergirded with the awareness of the Caring Presence. I will rely heavily upon them, and count them as my mentors, but I will regard them as one of two converging streams.

So, I truly believe that how we listen depends greatly upon what we think is happening in the other person. I affirm that weaving the contributions of those who have valued the listening process with the richness of the one who has given us an *abba-imma* theology will bring forth most sacred and beautiful results.

I want now to show how a theology of listening works. So far I have been speaking of our longing to be heard and a reason for listening in Jesus and recent theology. Now I wish to set the stage by painting a picture of a valley and describing a family who lives there. They will be the illustrations. As always, that which is abstract must become specific somewhere. We now turn to people who live in a particular place who both need to be heard and need to listen.

Hills surround Wenatchee. In whichever direction I scan the horizon, I must look up—"I will lift up mine eyes...." To the north, Burch Mountain, the south, Saddle Rock, the east, Badger Mountain, and the west, Castle Rock, all give silent testimony to an earlier era. Below the skyline are wilderness areas of rock, sage, and scattered pine trees meeting the ever-present orchards. Neighborhoods have encroached on the orchards and two small communities nestle on the banks of the mighty Columbia River. The serene and peaceful scene that I see today gives little clue to the tumultuous and cataclysmic events that gave rise to this present-day valley.

The earth cracked open and spewed forth molten lava some six to sixteen million years ago.[12] Over two hundred flows covered the earlier tropical forest to a depth of one to two miles of black basalt. The small, fully preserved rhinoceros found in one of the air bubbles of the lava stream witnesses to that lush primordial era. The largest lava flow in all of North America covered northern Idaho, eastern Oregon, and central Washington, finally ending at the Pacific Ocean.

The Columbia Plateau came into being. The gradual cooling and ponderous weight of this massive basalt formation led to a sinking of the inner circle, like the cooling of a warm pudding, creating the present-day Columbia Basin. The rim of the basin was left with an elevation of two to four thousand feet while the center sunk to five hundred feet. The prehistoric Columbia River had been pushed to the north and west by the lava flow. This, however, was to change dramatically during the Ice Age and would form the base for this present day valley.

Large ice sheets surged southward over a two million year period, advancing into and receding from this basin. During the final advance, a large glacier created a dam across a river in northern Montana, the tiny beginning of the Columbia River.[13] An expansive reservoir resulted, Lake Missoula, with a depth of two thousand feet and a length of two hundred miles.

At some critical point the water level overran the ice dam, lifting and carrying it from its grounding with unbelievable force. A wall of water from five hundred to one thousand feet high roared westward at the speed of up to fifty miles per hour. Following the lower levels of the basalt basin, the massive flow cut, ripped, and tore its way across three states, carrying with it massive boulders, sand, and soil.

Once would have been cataclysmic, but the lake was dammed, filled, and emptied as many as forty times in a period between 15,000 and 12,800 years ago. Time and again massive coulees were cut into the earlier laid basalt rock, reshaping the entire terrain. Thus was formed the winding valley along the entire Columbia River and that particular valley known today as Wenatchee. The serenity of the river today, quieted by the Grand Coulee and a series of lesser dams, and the beauty of the orchards on the hillsides belie the massive disruptions that called them into being.

The original humans in this valley were probably the Clovis people. A recent archaeological dig, located in an orchard near the airport, disclosed artifacts dating approximately eleven thousand years ago, shortly after the great cataclysmic floods. Of course, any evidence of human life in this region before that date would likely have been summarily swept into the Pacific Ocean. Here beneath these sloping hills, where now we farm, the early Americans fished, hunted, and gathered.

Europeans arrived over a century ago, having come first to an area northwest of Wenatchee, christening their frontier village, "Mission!" Those who settled in this present community retained the name given by the Yakima Indians: "Wenatchi: river flowing from canyon."[14] The city of Wenatchee was incorporated December 23, 1892.

Whatever we do, even listening, is located in a particular setting of land, flora, fauna, community, and history. Indeed, often our environment pervades that for which we long and yearn. The backdrop is now set for our story of one family.

Sue grew up in Seattle, a city girl; Don was raised in Wenatchee, a country boy. They met in college and married when both were seniors. Into this union they brought both their love and their differences. From the beginning Sue felt destined to be a teacher. Her mother had taught after Sue and her younger sister, Judy, entered high school. Her father had worked in the Bremerton Shipyards during World War II, when Sue was born. He later found a job with Boeing building airplanes rather than ships.

Besides her strong desire to be a teacher, Sue was determined in another way. She vowed to see another side of life, and so had decided much earlier that she would attend Washington State University, located in a rural area across the state from her home. So it was that she lived in a large women's residence hall, worked part-time in the university library, and attended a community church in Pullman. She thrived on her new life, her excitement increasing as she had more opportunities to observe and teach children. Her sense that she was a natural-born teacher was affirmed.

In her outgoing and caring way, she became acquainted with a young man in the student group of her church. He was an "Ag" student, from the central part of the state, majoring in horticulture, a term she had never heard before. Don had decided on the "other university" for quite different reasons than Sue. It was the only college where he could study to become an educated orchardist. His two years in the Air Force had helped him to realize that he missed the apple trees among which he had been raised. Originally he had enlisted to get away from the valley and experience new adventures.

On returning he had talked with his parents about his newfound awareness: "East, West, home is best!" They were surprised and pleased, since Don was the only one of their three sons who considered settling here. It was agreed that Don would manage and later buy their apple and pear orchards when they retired. With this sense of direction, Don sought an education, knowing what he wanted to do but not knowing if he could manage the array of science and math classes leading him to his goal. He did know, however, that orcharding was in his blood. After all, he was a third-generation orchardist from the Wenatchee valley.

When in love, you know who you want to live with, not necessarily where you want to live, and so it was with Don and Sue. It became an issue late in their courtship as they prepared for their Christmas wedding in Seattle and their graduation to follow a short five months later. One guideline became clear: You may find a teaching position just about anywhere in the state of Washington, but positions in the fruit industry are most available along the Columbia River winding through the center of the state.

Job interviews came from Wenatchee, and not surprisingly interviewers knew Don's family. It seemed a foregone conclusion, as Sue was offered a position as a third-grade teacher at Lewis and Clark Elementary School in Wenatchee. Don would be the newest field manager for Columbia Orchards. The newly married, newly graduated couple came to build their lives in this small city outlined with fruit trees beside a wide river.

But that was twenty-four years ago, and much has happened in that time span. They decided to have children after Sue had taught three years, and in due time there arrived a daughter, Kathy, and three years later a son, Brad. After first living in a rental home, Don's parents offered them an acre of ground on one of the orchards. They built their own home, doing much of the finishing work themselves. Sue had reservations about living so close to her in-laws, but learned to get along after some difficult moments and some unspoken agreements.

When Brad was in the seventh grade, Sue decided it was time for her to return to teaching and found a second-grade class at the Sunnyslope School. While she had enjoyed parenting, it was good for her to be back in a setting that she found natural and fulfilling. During this time, Don was promoted to assistant manager of the firm, after filling a variety of positions along the way. It was understood that he was being groomed to be manager and this promotion was merely a matter of time.

Don had kept involved in the orchard, first by leasing and later buying fifteen acres. Within five years his parents would retire and he would manage their remaining land. Busy but happy was the watchword for his present lifestyle. In fact, it would apply for both Sue and Don.

As we enter into the life of this family, their situation unfolds as follows. Kathy is a senior at Pacific Lutheran University, soon to graduate. Brad has just graduated from Wenatchee High School and is spending the summer on a Forest Service fire-fighting crew at a base camp in Twisp, about three hours north. Sue has completed her application for an internship for adminstrator's credentials and plans to begin that program in the fall. Don plans to become manager of the firm within the next few months and remain in that position for about ten years to gain a higher retirement pension, then give full time to managing the family orchard.

Their family is active in a community church of about three hundred members, located within an easy drive of their home. Needless to say, on their arrival this young couple was warmly welcomed into the congregation and eagerly invited to serve as counselors of the youth group.

Over the years Sue has taught in nearly every grade level of the church school, while Don has served as scout master of the church's troop, as well as a trustee and a member of the administrative council. Sue joined the preschool mother's group and has moved through the parenting years with them, while Don has been a member of the men's morning Bible study group for years.

It is into this situation that we enter their lives. We will learn how listening to others and being listened to by others affects them. They are not persons from abusive families who have led conflict-laden lives, nor are they totally fulfilled and satisfied in daily life. Don and Sue are, rather, more typical members of a family who can at times offer the gift of listening and at times are in dire need of that gift.

The next chapter opens with an unexpected happening that brings them both into a longing to be heard.

Notes

[1] Edward Robinson, *Original Vision: A Study of the Religious Experience of Childhood* (New York: The Seabury Press, 1983).

[2] Joachim Jeremias, *The Prayers of Jesus* (Philadelphia: Fortress Press, 1967).

[3] *Ibid.*, p. 14.

[4]*Ibid.*, p. 25.

[5]*Ibid.*, p. 59.

[6]*Ibid.*, p. 56.

[7]*Ibid.*, p. 60.

[8]*Ibid.*, p. 29.

[9]See John B. Cobb, Jr., and David Ray Griffin, *Process Theology: An Introductory Exposition* (Philadelphia: Westminster Press, 1976).

[10]Carl Rogers, *Client-centered Therapy* (Boston: Houghton Mifflin, 1951).

[11]Thomas Gordon, *Parent Effectiveness Training* (New York: Peter H. Wyden, Inc., 1970).

[12]John Eliot Allen, Marjorie Burns, and Sam C. Sargent, *Cataclysms on the Columbia* (Portland, Oregon: Timber Press, 1986), p. 77.

[13]*Ibid.*, p. 103.

[14]James W. Phillips, *Washington State Place Names* (Seattle: University of Washington Press, 1971), p. 157.

2

Blossoming from Bud to Flower

"Pray then in this way:
Our Father in heaven, hallowed be
your name...."

Matthew 6:9

Behold, a rose bud blossoms into a flower! This wondrous blossoming is the image I have chosen to illustrate the basic form of listening. Blossoming captures what is happening in listening.

The bud represents the first words spoken. In the situation ahead with Sue and Don they are, "I'm just down in the dumps" and "I'm between a rock and a hard place." In both we do not yet know the particular flowers that may come forth from those buds. Many are possible. We can only be sure that something will likely blossom.

It is this blossoming that will be described here. We begin with a speaker who longs to be heard. The reasons to speak are often from anguish: yearning, pain, hurt, confusion, or indecision. But they can just as easily be from joy: excitement, happiness, accomplishment, or ecstasy. The bud is the beginning of something that cries out to be shared.

Just as necessary is the listener, the other partner in the blossoming process. The listener's role, in my understanding, is twofold: *reflecting* and *waiting with caring*. While these may appear simple, they are the basics. Here is where we start.

Reflecting is sharing back what is said. That can be described in a variety of ways: mirror, say it back, give feedback, follow along, go with the other, or walk in their shoes. Specific examples of doing so may take one of the following forms: "It sounds like you...," "I hear you saying...," "So, you're...," "You're really feeling...." These are the specific skills that have been given to us by Rogers and Gordon.

These phrases may truly sound strange and stilted, and so they should. To help another person blossom is to enter into a strange new world. This world is radically different than the "put-downs" and "zingers" we hear so often on television sitcoms or read on greeting cards. Though we may feel on unfamiliar ground in reflecting, we have entered the world of grace.

The second activity is to *wait with caring*. It sounds so easy, yet it can be so hard. The task is to wait for the next utterance of words from the speaker. Being quiet permits and promotes blossoming. By waiting, we express curiosity about the particular way the speaker will allow the flower to open rather than the way we might say it. Waiting allows the speaker to search for and find words.

Several images may help to show what is happening in the waiting: allowing the other to put it into words, transforming the wordless into words, changing the invisible into the visible, encouraging an inner search, traveling with the other on an adventure, or going from here to there. All involve expectant waiting.

The ways in which the speaker tells what is happening may take several forms: "Let's see, how can I say it...," "Words seem to fail me...," "I don't know how to get it across...," "I'm looking for the right words...," "That didn't come out like I thought it would...," "It's hard to describe, but its kinda like...."

The longing to be heard pushes the search for words. The need to be understood will not allow it to go unspoken. Waiting allows this blossoming to unfold. We cannot do it for the speaker. We can only encourage his or her process. Later I will focus more upon God's part in this blossoming process, but for now let it be said that God is creating with the speaker. Words are formed from no words. Creation is occurring just as surely as God's creation of a universe and a people!

Listening is reflecting and waiting with caring. The first two activities have been described. Now I wish to speak of *caring*. The attitude we hold toward the speaker is of utmost importance. Since much of the vital information we give to another about ourselves is from the language of our bodies, rather than from the words we speak, a caring stance is essential.

Several words that may help to describe caring are: patient, gentle, interested, curious, expectant, and receptive. Strangely, these words begin to sound like those found in the letters of Paul.

A term that has emerged among professionals who listen is *empathy*, a feeling along with the other person. I affirm the need for empathy that is intertwined with the mystery and awe expressed in Exodus. Moses, approaching the awesome burning bush, is told to remove his shoes for the ground he stands upon is sacred ground (Exodus 3:5). The blossoming process is, likewise, sacred ground. Creation is occuring!

Above all, I have experienced the listening process as one of mystery, and I am convinced that God is at the heart of this mystery. Here, the knowledge that *abba-imma* is present is crucial. It characterizes the uniqueness of this approach to listening.

We are not always accurate in reflecting what the speaker says, but it is important that our hearts be in the right place. If we wait with caring, the speaker will correct us and the relationship will remain strong. Belief that there is a Presence, an *abba-imma*, in the listening process empowers the decision to wait with caring.

To summarize the blossoming process, a speaker yearns to be heard and is moved to put things into words, while the listener reflects as accurately as possible what is heard, then waits with caring for the next words to come forth as the speaker struggles to create words out of no words. Reflecting, waiting, and caring are the foundation!

Now I wish to turn to the qualities of blossoming. Again, images guide my way of speaking of that which is both mysterious and complex. Blossoming implies an opening, a coming forth, a change, a process, and a movement.

Blossoming is an unfolding, small to large; an expanding, narrow to wide; a growing, simple to complex; a clarifying, vague to clear; an identifying, unnamed to named; a sensitizing, numb to intense; a deepening, shallow to deep; a seeing, invisible to visible; an integrating, separated to connected; and a knowing, unknown to known.

Blossoming is only one image and, like a parable, has only one point. The image differs from an allegory, which would find some meaning in each phase of the bud becoming flower. Images simply point toward, but cannot adequately capture, some greater reality. In this case, the reality is a creative process.

To listen is to engage in a mysterious creative process. Often within this process is found the heart's desire of the speaker and somewhere, hidden in the depths, are intimations of God's heart's desire for that person.

I affirm that God is an encouraging presence within this blossoming, as the speaker struggles to put into words that which is now only experience. The basic results of the blossoming are powerful: to understand oneself more fully, and to be understood more fully by another. If only this basic step occurs, I proclaim this is a healing process!

At times when blossoming does not occur, the creative process is thwarted. Those actions of the listener that frequently inhibit the growth are questioning, probing, and interrogating, which carry with them the sense of force, pressure, and control. Equally prohibitive are telling the speaker what is best, safe, or right and explaining what the speaker should feel, want, or do.

The constructive, creative struggle to find for oneself where his or her heart's desires lie and where *abba-imma* may call them is lost. Nurturing the blossoming, by contrast, is a gentle process.

I want to illustrate the blossoming process, by showing how it works with two particular persons. All this "flowery" language must come down to one "rose." We turn to Sue. Her bud, as noted earlier, is "I'm down in the dumps." At this point no one knows the qualities of her flower, yet to come. It is as yet a mysterious unknown.

We will be observing to see how Sue's friends reflect and wait with caring. We should not expect them to be experts and always do it just right, but rather watch to see the caring position they take with Sue. My hope is that they will help her to experience the awareness that comes with blossoming.

It is summer in Wenatchee. The light wisp of green that graced the hills and the splotches of yellow balsam flowers have turned to brown. The whites and pinks of orchard blossoms have passed. Don is busy helping to manage a fruit warehouse. Sue is taking summer classes to keep her teaching credentials current.

Let us eavesdrop on Sue's sharing group in the church, made up of women who have met regulary for a number of years. The meeting is nearly over on this Wednesday morning.

Joan: Is something wrong, Sue? You've been so quiet today.

Sue: Well, I don't know what to say. I guess I'm down in the dumps.

Gayle: Let's hear about it. That's what this group is all about.

Sue: Oh, I feel guilty starting now. Our time is almost up. I don't want to keep you.

Rosa: No problem for me. Groceries can be bought later.

Anne: My kids are at the neighbors, having a great time.

Sue: OK...well...I feel on the verge of tears all the time. And here I go right now...I promised myself...I don't want to fall apart today.

Pam: Crying's OK with me. We've all done our share.

Joan: Crying helps.

Sue: I can't quite put my finger on what's wrong. That's part of why I'm so upset. I suppose it's lots of things. My life's not going the way I thought it would.

Anne: You mean the real thing isn't like you planned it.

Sue: Not at all! Just when Don and I could relax a little and have some fun I find out Dad's failing badly...I'm just worried sick about him.

Rosa: No wonder you're down in the dumps.

Gayle: I know what that's like!

Sue: Mom told me she's been concerned for some time...but couldn't get Dad to a doctor. He just kept saying he was fine and a little vacation would fix him up. She got him there and his health looks even worse than she had thought.

Pam: Oh, Sue, I'm so sorry!

Joan: Oh, my!

Anne: I can see why you feel like crying.

Sue: Well...thanks. I guess...it's nice to hear you say it's OK to cry and feel bad. I...don't know how to tell you what I'm feeling....I guess...I feel scared! Yeah...scared down to the tips of my toes. I can't believe it! Can this be happening to my dad, always so healthy and alert? And only seventy.

Rosa: Hard to believe.

Gayle: And frightening.

Sue: And I'm so frustrated! What can I do? They're three hours away. Don's in his busy season and I'm in my third week of summer school. I just can't stand the thought of Mom dealing with this all by herself...but Judy's way down in San Diego. I want to go, but it's so hard to work around schedules...and I don't want to go alone.

Anne: You need to go, but it's hard to see a way to do it.

Sue: I've been worrying myself sick lately. I can't come up with a plan that seems to work. I try to talk with Don, but he's under a lot of pressure with his job.

Pam: You're left to deal with all this stress by yourself.

Sue: You're right! I'm alone. I hadn't put it that way before, but I have felt all alone. I'm lonely for my dad...and who knows how much of him I'll ever have again? And...lonely for Don and he isn't there.

Joan: That's loneliness all the way around.

Sue: Yes...the ones I'm closest to and turned to the most....I need to get over there and see Dad. No...that's not enough! I need to hold him and cry with him...and what have we got? Big weddings these next two weekends and a term paper due in two weeks.

Rosa: You are in a terrible bind.

Sue: I feel that bind. I'm trying to be patient, but I haven't done too well. I haven't even told the kids yet. They've got enough to handle without this and I don't know quite what to tell them, really.

Gayle: It's tough to carry the load all by yourself.

Sue: And I don't want to carry it alone! I'm tired of it! It's hard to admit, but I've been angry at Don. For heaven's sake, that's not what I want. I want to be close, especially now....But every time I try to push those angry feelings away, back they come.

Joan: You don't want to be angry, but you are.

Sue: Yes! I don't like to say it, but I am. He doesn't need me feeling this way....He's so upset anyway, but I guess I've done all the giving. I've lived on the same orchard with his folks since Kathy was little. Well, the other day I tried to get him to talk about the possibility of moving closer to Dad and Mom. He just looked away and never said a word!

Anne: It must feel unfair to you after all you've done for Don.

Pam: No wonder you're resentful.

Sue: I am, but I don't want to be. I start feeling guilty right away, thinking I'm too hard on him. I go around and around. I wish I could get this all straightened out in my mind. But he's just so shut down with me.

Joan: You resent the way Don ignores you, then you get down on yourself.

Sue: Can't he see that I need him close to me, most of all right now? Doesn't he know I need comfort? I don't want to fight with him. I want to talk with him.

Gayle: You must feel deeply hurt.

Sue: That's it. I do feel hurt. That's right! Doubly hurt.

Rosa: So, hurt is what you feel most.

Sue: Exactly, I knew I was angry...but somehow I felt there was something more....It really hurts!

Pam: So...hurt's at the bottom.

Sue:	I guess I expected Don to be my rock. I could lean on him and he'd do what I've done for him so many times. It's my turn, but he's not there. I want him to be, but he's just not. That's painful!
Anne:	Oh, Sue! You deserve better!
Sue:	I can even feel that pain…right here in my heart. Oh!…Like my heart is breaking!…
Rosa:	I'd like to hold your hand.
Gayle:	Me, too. I'm here for you.
Sue:	Whoa! I almost lost control there…OK…now I'm OK.
Pam:	Those are strong feelings!
Sue:	Are they ever!…But, I'm all right….Strange…but I even feel better now.
Joan:	Good.
Rosa:	Wonderful!
Anne:	Glad for you!
Sue:	I never thought I had all that in me. It's so good to let it out….Thanks, friends. Thanks for caring!

Sue had reason to be down in the dumps! She was truly needful. After an initial encouragement to speak, she poured out her heart. Her friends responded in short, summary phrases, following as best they could what Sue said in each statement, then waiting. Neither they nor we could have guessed beforehand what direction Sue would go. It only became more clear as Sue created words.

Because Sue was deeply distressed, she did not focus on the mirroring itself that was being offered by her friends. Rather she struggled to put thoughts and feelings into spoken words and heard herself say those words. Then she heard them a second time, as others offered their understanding of her thoughts and feelings back to her. In this movement, her inner experiences became real, not daydreams or fantasies. Now, for the first time, she has words with which to work, tools to build something, rather than a jumble of confusion within.

The bud was being down in the dumps, the flower a profound hurt that Don was distant during her crisis. The pain was identified and named. It became clear, likewise, that her pain was appropriate. This much was done and was healing, even though no solution has yet been found. There was, rather, a beginning. Much is left unfinished. With a confidence that God is present in this process, Sue will certainly continue the healing work she has now begun.

The blossoming of the bud for Sue revealed three important arenas: persons, circumstances, and feelings. We can be quite certain that by listening we will hear about relationships with important people. Therein is where most of our agony and ecstasy is centered. From Sue, we heard an expanding list of names: Dad, Mom, Judy, Kathy, Don, and Don's folks. Intensity was felt first with Dad, then with Don. Blossoming will tell us who's there.

The circumstances widened like an expanding circle. The Latin origin of *circumstance* is helpful: *stance*, standing, and *circum*, around. We listen for who and what is "standing around." For Sue, they widened from Dad's health, to barriers to visiting her folks, to the unfulfilled need to share with Don. These unfolding dramas provide the action of the people in her life.

Finally, Sue has feelings interwoven with the circumstances she faces with people important to her. They, too, expand and change. Sue is sad, tearful, confused, scared, frustrated, lonely, resentful, guilty, put upon, and hurt. There is a flow into a feeling, experiencing and naming it, then moving on to another.

Her discovery was hurt, which felt more basic than the earlier unfairness and resentment. Her physical sensations accompanying the hurt cried out its importance. The central point is the movement and flow from one to another. Such is blossoming.

Blossoming reveals the heart's desires of Sue: who

she loves, what is happening with them, and how she responds. Feelings and decisions interweave with persons and circumstances. Blossoming is movement, process, change. Blossoming is creating.

As her friends listened and reflected, they named, affirmed, and accepted her thoughts and feelings. By doing this, Sue went on to something new. She did not simply stay in one place, repeating: "I'm scared!" "I'm scared!" "I'm scared!" Her attention moved, her focus changed, new persons were named, new circumstances emerged, new feelings appeared. A process was occurring. She was going from here to there.

For Sue, her particular blossoming was an unfolding of feelings and experiencing the intensity of those feelings. She became aware of herself in ways she had not known before she spoke. Such awareness is essential for Sue to take productive action.

God, the *abba-imma* known by Jesus, must have been rejoicing. Within the church, friends helped another toward liberation. I heartily believe that God does rejoice in such a moment. Healing is always cause for celebration, but for me that does not say it strongly enough.

I affirm that God was actively involved in those events, stirring Sue to form each word she would utter and luring her friends to offer the gift of listening. Not once did anyone use the name of God. Nevertheless, by their responses they were in deep cooperation with God's mission.

So, we leave our first encounter with blossoming, one of the gifts of listening. Let us now take our learning and apply it to a second event. Hopefully, some of the original strangeness may fade and the next dialogue will feel more familiar. Don is on the other side of Sue's loneliness and hurt. He seeks out a friend he has known for years through the Thursday morning Bible study group. We have permission to listen in.

Don: Thanks for taking the time to have a cup of coffee with me.

John: Glad to do it, Don.

Don: I sure feel like I'm between a rock and a hard place!

John: It sounds bad.

Don: As if I didn't have enough to handle, Sue's upset with me. I'm really afraid to talk with her.

John: Like you'll get into some hot water.

Don: You know better than anyone how I've been all churned up about this job thing. I hate that stupid Alar scare!

John: Right! We've all lived with that one day and night.

Don: If apples were selling right now, I'd be sitting pretty. Here I am in the same old job and I know Sue will use that to say, "Let's move to Seattle."

John: So that's what you're afraid to talk about.

Don: Yeah, I can hear her now. "OK, Don, it's a good time to leave. You didn't get the promotion, our kids are in college, my dad is failing, and Mom needs my help. Let's go!"

John: She's got a good argument.

Don: A good one for her, but I just can't do it. I can't even talk about it.

John: You dread facing it.

Don: Yes, that's what's so hard. I feel for her too. I'm not numb. I wouldn't wish sickness and old age on anybody. I know she needs to help out her folks.

John: Of course, you can see her side of it, too.

Don: That's exactly what puts me in the bind. I don't want to go toe-to-toe with her, when I know she's already feeling hurt. But I'm not very proud of myself when I just keep quiet, thinking it'll all blow over for a while.

John: You feel like you can't win.

Don: Right! That's my theme song lately. You know, I really looked forward to this time in my life....I thought I'd have the new job, the kids would be on their own, and we'd have more time for ourselves....No more hot dog feeds, piano recitals, football games, or driving lessons.

John: Seems like you've been cheated.

Don: Sure feels like it. It hasn't come out the way I had it planned. I feel gypped! So, who do I blame?....Who do I yell at?

John: You do need somebody to blame.

Don: I wish it'd all go away. I'm sure confused! I used to be able to think straight, but now I keep playing tricks on myself, like...watch this:...I say, "maybe her dad's health may not turn out as bad as they think." But we've already seen some of his problems. I really dread going over there. It just brings having to deal with Sue that much closer.

John: You'd like to wish away the problem, but you can't.

Don: I do know that, John. I've even asked myself if I could take Seattle. Good grief, my job is here, my folks, the orchard, all our friends,...the open spaces, the hills, the river. Do you know that I've only been away from this valley for six years since I was born here? I belong here! I can't pull up my roots. There's gotta be some other way!

John: You love it here. That's clear.

Don: But then, that's exactly what Sue did for me. The city girl came to the country. She gave up things for me. She's got every right to ask me to return the favor. That's where I get myself in trouble. I want to be fair to her, but I want to live in my home country....Maybe I can't have both.

John: There's the rock and the hard place!

Don: Yes! I keep swinging around to this Alar thing. If that scare hadn't come along, I'd be set in the new job and Sue probably wouldn't ever ask me to leave. But here I go again. I've already spent weeks riding that merry-go-round. It does no good. It's over! It's done! Let go of it!

John: You're still angry about missing out on your new job.

Don: Its hard to let go of what I wanted. I still have my dream! Then I kick myself and say, "Get with the program!"

John: You're right. That dream is really powerful.

Don: You know I've always prided myself on being practical, a guy who deals with whatever comes along. But on this one, I think I'm still the dreamer.

John: This is a real test for you.

Don: So, it's not going to go away. Guess I'll have to face what has really happened....Yeah, what's happening.

John: Sounds hard.

Don: OK, if I'm going to face it...then I better do what I've been dreading. I need to see her dad for myself. Then I'll start those long talks with Sue.

John: First you do need to see him for yourself.

Don: I do. For Pete's sake, I know I'm a good thinker and so is Sue. Actually we've done pretty well together through the years. Maybe we could find some way out of this mess. I guess I'd better hear her out before I jump to any conclusions about a move.

John: Start, maybe, by listening to her.

Don: Well, it sure couldn't be any worse than tuning her out like I've been doing....Now wait...here's an idea....Yeah....How does this sound to you, John? I'd talk with her now about what she's going through, but say let's not make any plans yet.

John: Talk about feelings now and plans later.

Don: Sure! That's probably what she needs...and I know it would be a big weight off my shoulders.

John: Yeah, a relief for both of you!

Don: Maybe that will work! It might go a long way toward closing the gap between us. I could do that.

John: Great! Let me know how it's going. I'll be thinking about you.

Once again the listener reflected and waited with caring, trusting that Don would find his own solution. A trust is placed in the divine lure toward harmony that is present in all of us. A strange new language, made up of short mirroring statements, was the method. The two sides of his dilemma were clarified. Then, in a surprising manner a solution emerged.

In contrast to Sue's blossoming by clarifying her feelings, Don's centered more on identifying his problem. Instead of the new awareness, "I feel hurt," Don discovered, "I can do something." His process led him to a new decision about the kind of person he could become next.

Don had been avoiding the dreaded task of talking with Sue. He had not been able to deal with this evasion by his usual method of thinking things out by himself. This should be no surprise, since tough issues are hard to face alone. From Gethsemane we hear the poignant question, "Could you not keep awake one hour?"(Mark 14:37b). The answer for Don was the presence of a caring person who honored his need to struggle toward his own solution.

Once again, we can use the perspectives of people, circumstances, and feelings to review Don's talking. Don spoke of fewer people than Sue, focusing primarily on her, while her dad and their children hovered in the background. Actually, the primary person in his talk was Don, himself, struggling with himself. In listening, we never know quite where the focus will be—the inner voices of the speaker or the wider relationships with others.

Several important circumstances emerged: losing a job promotion due to the Alar scare, avoiding talking with Sue because of fear she will want to move, and fighting between a need to be fair to Sue and a need to stay in his home country.

Don's feelings accompanied his discussion of the people and the circumstances: trapped, afraid, angry, torn, guilty, cheated, dreading, and satisfied. Feelings did not play the central role for Don that they had for Sue. Rather they were more attached to his past actions and the newly proposed action.

The solution found is fragile. We have no certainty that Don will talk with Sue, or how it will go if he does. Often in listening this is all we get.

Just enough light to see a short distance ahead on the trail is often all of God's mysterious guidance that the speaker may receive in any given moment. Don sensed a tiny fragile possibility leading toward harmony, though he registers no awareness of the one who calls him to harmony. I must admit that this is a far cry from knowing God's will for one's entire life. Still, as a listener, it is important to be satisfied with this one small step.

The two dialogues have shown the fundamental form of listening, blossoming from bud to flower. It is simple and basic, the foundation for all that will follow. The foundation is built upon a trust in a process occurring within the speaker, an intimate relationship with a Caring Presence who offers new direction. Grounded in this trust, it is possible to offer reflecting and waiting with care.

Now I wish to share what I think is happening with Don and Sue in this listening process. The focus here is not upon the content of their speaking, but upon a theory of listening itself. Four concepts are necessary: experience, awareness, words, and feelings. This theory proposes that persons increase their awareness of their own experiences by putting them into words. Let us begin with the meaning of experience.

We are experiencing constantly, most of which is not in our awareness. Our hearts beat, our eyes blink, our throats swallow, our lungs inhale and exhale, our ears register sound waves, our stomachs digest, and our cramped legs quietly "go to sleep." Unless our attention is called to these events, we are not aware of their occurring. Experiences are wider than awareness.

We do become aware when experiences are intense and dramatic. Sharp hunger pangs strike, drowsy eyelids become heavy, and rapid heart beats of "flight or fight" shock us.

Just as we experience body sensations, so we have only limited awareness of feelings. We may have learned to identify our anger, but not recognize our fear; become quite familiar with sadness, but be oblivious to loneliness; known well the pangs of guilt, but not have named our hurt; and acknowledged our excitement, but never voiced our awe.

Once again, strong feelings are likely to intrude into our awareness, but even then may appear labeled incorrectly. We always feel more than we know we feel.

Likewise, we experience our relationships with the environment with little accompanying awareness. Temperature is frequently unknown until it becomes very hot or very cold, humidity is attended to only if it moves to high or low extremes. Downpours and thunderstorms usually gain our attention more than the ordinary blue sky. The familiar bird song of the English sparrow may go unheard while the distinctive call of the California quail may pierce our awareness.

For most of us, dramatic happenings in the lives of loved ones living several hundred miles away are out of our consciousness. Some among us, however, are so sensitive as to feel immediately and intensely the exact second when an accident or a death occurs to a family member.

We experience our own past, but usually are not aware of doing so. Long-held unspoken beliefs that we must accomplish to be lovable, or must please others to be acceptable, may be dictating our present actions. A long-forgotten vow to never put ourselves in a postion to be hurt again may be guiding what we do in the moment. We do not know it. We simply carry out what seems natural.

Finally, it is my conviction that we also experience God in every moment, but seldom are we aware of God's presence. Some may be able to recall special moments of wondrous revelation, but not know God in their ordinary events. More often we vaguely sense God's possibilities for us, but not the Giver of those possibilities. Again, our experience of the Divine is deeper and wider than our awareness.

So, starting with our multitude of experiences, we struggle to increase our awareness of them by forming them into words. Naming by words increases awareness, and words always come interwoven with feeling. While a precise scientific lecture does not carry the same type or intensity of feelings as a love poem by Elizabeth Barrett Browning, still I affirm there are feelings in both.

Certainly those words spoken from a longing to be heard come wrapped with inseparable feelings. Those feelings expressed without words, such as flowing tears, need to be shaped into words. They are a part of our reservoir of experience calling for awareness.

Listening is a creative process, then, by which one helps another to increase awareness of experiences by struggling with that person for the appropriate words to express them. Listening allows and affirms the necessary struggle, often painful, that leads to increasing satisfaction.

Listening expands our awareness of life, which I affirm to be good. Surely only a small segment of life is exposed in any one hearing: a value, a relationship, a feeling, a memory, or a new direction. Most of all it is good to become increasingly aware of that *abba-imma* relationship that continually lures us to love. Knowing our calling and who calls us is best. Listening promotes this!

This theory may be applied now to Sue and Don to see from a wider perspective what was happening as they spoke. Sue was having a "merry-go-round" of experiences, primarily feelings. She knew that she was "down," but not much more. Whatever feelings were present were vague and unspoken, constantly swirling within her mind.

What is crucial is that as she began to talk, the unspoken became spoken. Searching for words was slow and arduous, expanding from one feeling more widely into another. From "around and around," she progressed to "going somewhere" as good friends patiently heard her out and spoke back to her.

She went wider and wider into her experiences until she named that feeling that most genuinely described who she was at that time. Thinking to oneself is dramatically different than speaking aloud to others.

Don was experiencing a bind and those feelings that accompany such a dilemma. His speaking allowed him to find words to describe the two important values that had him trapped: fairness to Sue and love for his valley. Often he did not know where he was going as he verbally surveyed the barriers forming the bind.

There had to be some "milling around" in order to gradually express with increasing clarity where he stood and what surrounded him. As clarity emerged, the stage was set for the possiblity of a new answer to the formerly impossible situation.

The particular quality of blossoming that seems to be present with Don is *clarifying*: from vague to clear. For Sue the quality was one of *expanding*: from narrow to wide.

I have shared the basic form of listening: reflecting, and waiting with caring. The content of listening is most often people, circumstances, and feelings. The purpose is to increase awareness of experiences by putting them into words that carry feeling. Listening is undergirded by faith in an *abba-imma* relationship deep within this mysterious process that is made manifest in both direction and presence.

Having come this far, I now offer an invitation. Come, join me in offering the gift of listening to others. Yes, it sounds strange. Yes, it feels funny. Yes, it may be embarrassing. Yet, the possibilities are wondrous. The fields are ripe for harvest. So many hunger and yearn to be heard, especially those whom we love most. We can make such a difference with relatively little effort.

In the church we have a rich treasure. Whenever we gather, we pray, "Our Father…"! Herein we have a constant reminder of the relationship that undergirds us every moment. Our regular remembrance of *abba-imma* empowers us to offer the grace that comes forth when we listen.

Come, join me in a great adventure!

3

Walking in Another's Garden

*"I thank you, Father, Lord of heaven
and earth, because you have hidden
these things from the wise and the
intelligent and have revealed them
to infants; yes, Father, for such was
your gracious will. All things have
been handed over to me by my
Father; and no one knows who the
Son is except the Father, or who the
Father is except the Son and anyone
to whom the Son chooses to reveal
him."*

Luke 10:21–22

There are many kinds of gardens, which is one reason why I chose the image to illustrate the second type of listening. A vegetable garden is green and lush in its own way, but truly different from the colorful array of a rose garden. Both are, nonetheless, beautiful. Likewise, people, though different, exhibit their own colorful beauty.

The year I spent in New Mexico awakened me to a radically different sense of beauty than I had known in the Snake River Canyon of southern Idaho. I remember the delight of experiencing the tropical atmosphere of Florida's Cypress Gardens for the first time. How different it was from our own Ohme Gardens, a mosaic of evergreens surrounding green ponds, themselves encircled

43

by multi-colored flower beds providing homes for California quail and scampering chipmunks.

The variety is endless: formal European gardens, rich English herb gardens, manicured Japanese gardens, cactus gardens, rose gardens, tulip fields, vegetable gardens, tropical gardens, and rock gardens. So are our human lives endless in their variety. Perhaps I am so keenly aware of this varied beauty because in my usual day I listen to six to eight persons, rapidly shifting from one to the next after each hour. I have long considered myself to be walking in another's garden. When we listen, then, we are called upon to appreciate a diversity of beauty, not merely a single form of beauty. This becomes our challenge.

A second and equally compelling reason for choosing the image of a garden is that all gardens have variety within them. I have yet to see a garden that is total beauty. After all, there does need to be a compost pile somewhere. Looking carefully, we will usually find the unattractive areas.

There are the blighted plants, rock-laden areas, the sections of hard clay-like soil, the brownish stalks remaining from an earlier season, the ever-flourishing stand of weeds, the insect-infested branches, all amid the verdant, lush, multi-colored flowers. Likewise, after thirty-five years of listening to people, I know that all of us have unattractive parts as well.

A second challenge, then, is for us to listen to the unattractive parts of another person. It's easy to share and easy to hear the beautiful, agreeable, and pleasing. Not so with those words that display all of the garden—the contradictory, the unpleasant, the negative, the shameful, the despised, and the hidden parts. Hard to share? Yes. Hard to hear? Indeed!

If it is a gift to encourage bud to blossom, it is an even greater gift to listen to the unattractive and unacceptable parts of another. Such it is to walk in another's garden, all of the garden. So, variety abounds between gardens and within gardens. Being willing to "listen to it all" is the second important task before us if we will enter this ministry of God. Truly the challenge increases, but I can heartily witness from my own experience that the joys multiply even more. The paradox is that it is often in the unattractive that the gold is discovered.

To walk in another's garden, then, is to let that person take you by the hand and lead you to whatever he or she wants to show you. As listener you do not lead, nor do you point out something in the garden that the gardener has not yet shown you. The adventure is to follow with the trust that doing so will offer both you and the gardener some glimpse of where God is working in that garden. At times the walk is long and at times the glimpse is short, yet walking with another increases the possibilities of knowing God's presence.

Now I wish to move from the language of imagery to descriptive language. This form of listening is composed of two important tasks, the first is to follow the speaker and the second is to accept the changes in subject that the speaker makes. Clearly the second is a natural extension of the first. If you are truly following, you will turn corners when the speaker turns. The listener does not insist that the speaker finish a thought or stay with a subject until it is completely exhausted. The speaker is the tour guide.

I know that this sounds simple to do, and in a way it is. But in the midst of doing it, holding onto the arms of your chair or hanging onto your hat is often the urgent task. We will get a feel for that as we will shortly eavesdrop on Don listening to Sue.

The primary task remains, as we saw earlier: that of reflecting and waiting with care. All that is added now is to do so regardless of what the speaker is talking about. To the acts of reflecting and waiting with care, we add *following* and *changing*. The mission is to keep reflecting even if the topic turns to something very unpleasant or negative. It is precisely at this point that the speaker needs your understanding and acceptance the most.

We now turn to two illustrations, once again involving Don and Sue, as we follow them through the issues they face.

Late summer has turned to intimations of fall in the Wenatchee valley. This season brings browned, dry hills, earlier graced with a tender light green. The familiar beginnings of fruit harvest, school, and church activities harken another turn in our cycle of nature. A forest fire nearby has blackened thousands of acres of timber and grazing land. There is fear of deer starving up the Swakane Canyon due to the fire, and an equally frightening dread of drought ahead if the snow pack this winter is not deep enough in the higher elevations.

And Don musters his courage to talk to Sue, overcoming his own personal dread. Don had come to the conclusion in his talk with John that he might be able to handle talking with Sue about her feelings if there were no plans made. To make plans would be too distressing. After proposing this limitation to Sue, Don waited while Sue thought it over and he was pleased when she agreed.

We now overhear them as they are sitting at their breakfast room table over their second cup of coffee. Don will walk in Sue's garden.

Sue: OK, now, let me see if I have this straight. You're saying we can talk about anything, but not make any plans yet about what to do.

Don: Yes.

Sue: That means we won't even discuss when we can go to visit the folks or think about what we might do in the long run?

Don: That's what we agreed. I'd like to hear what you're feeling.

Sue: I know I agreed to it for your sake, so I'll do my best to stick to it. You're really afraid of what we'd get into if we did more?

Don: I hate to admit it, but that's right.

Sue: So what you really want to know is what I've been

going through since Mom called....Well...it's been quite a bundle. My feelings have covered the alphabet. I don't think any of the letters have been left out.

Don: You've had all kinds of feelings.

Sue: It's really hard to talk about them now because it seems like so many of the feelings have faded away, or maybe I've given up and buried them.

Don: Your feelings aren't fresh anymore.

Sue: They might be if I were talking with someone else, but Don, I've kind of become hardened to you. Sort of like I had to stagger around trying to carry this bundle all by myself.

Don: You felt I wasn't there for you.

Sue: That's putting it mildly. I felt your aloofness, like you didn't really care. I was alone.

Don: I left you facing it all alone.

Sue: Right! It's hard to get over that. But, I guess I should be glad that you finally want to talk. So, I'll try my best to tell you what I've been going through.

Don: Its very hard for you to talk to me after the way I've treated you.

Sue: I'll try being logical and objective. I can tell you like I was another person watching me....I've been worried sick. I haven't been able to keep my mind on anything, especially my classroom. I know the kids have suffered and I feel so guilty about that.

Don: It sounds like you've been filled with worry and it's kept you from doing your best work.

Sue: I don't know when I've forgotten more things and made more mistakes. Sometimes I'll catch myself driving to school when I was going after groceries. I have not been doing well.

Don: You can't seem to concentrate.

Sue: And I've felt so sad. You don't know the nights I've gotten out of bed and gone to the living room crying my eyes out. I can usually make it until about two in the morning, then I may never get back to sleep again.

Don: You've been crying a lot and not sleeping and I didn't even know it.

Sue: True, you have not asked. Who can say what it's all about? Part of it is that I just feel so lost and confused. I don't know what to do. What are you supposed to do when a person who has loved you and supported you whatever happened is not there to do that anymore?

Don: You're feeling lost without your dad's support.

Sue: Yes, and how lonely—how alone I have felt….That's the worst part of all this suffering. The kids are gone and I don't want to lean on them anyway…and you have been gone, too, in your own way.

Don: You've been terribly lonely without the kids or me.

Sue: Facing it alone is the worst! I have felt just awful…sick to my stomach…headaches…I can't do it alone. Oops!…Here come the buried feelings! I can't do this, Don! I simply can't talk this way! The feelings are too close.

Don: Those strong feelings are coming right now!

Sue: No, Don…no! I know what it is….I won't do it. I will not! Here we are doing it your way again. No, no….I just hate what we do!

Don: Wow! You're really mad at me!

Sue: Yes! So are you going to get up and walk away? Sure…go ahead…I'm used to it. That's what you always do when I get upset.

Don: No, I'm not going anywhere. It's hard, but I'm staying put!

Sue: OK then, hear me out. I have felt downright raw hatred toward you lately. I've had a smoldering anger toward you for a long time. Now I can name it.

Don: It sounds like you really do hate me right now!

Sue: Right!…Don, when I really deep down want something, you go quiet. That's when I hate you. You leave, you retreat somewhere.

Don: So you—

Sue: Stay back, Don. I need to finish this. I've needed to say it for a long time. I can tell when you don't agree…and don't want what I want. I never get an answer out of you. You are like…gone. I can read you now like a book. Then…get this…then I back off. What a fool I have been!

Don: You really hate me when I go quiet…and leave.

Sue: I hate it that you get your way. See, you can take it better than I can. I can't stand the gap between us, so I make up. Then you come back. But…but…I don't speak out what I wanted. It's lost! Somehow what I wanted in the beginning is lost in the shuffle. I give it up.

Don: You mean I get my way by going quiet.

Sue: Right! Do you know what you have been doing to me? First, I thought, *No, Don doesn't do it on purpose.* Now, I really think you do. You never have to struggle with me and you still end up getting your way. Such a deal!

Don: You've decided I manipulate you to get my way.

Sue: I see it now. I wish I had twenty years ago. It would have saved me a lot of heartache and quiet anger. I feel gypped! How stupid and naive I've been.

Don: So you feel I've duped you all these years.

Sue: Do I ever. And here I am about ready to sell my soul again. But hear me out, Don. There is no way that I will on this one. I won't let you control me about my folks. There's too much at stake here.

Don: I hear you. It's gonna be different this time.

Sue: To think that I agreed with you not to talk about plans. It's not that I can't, I won't....I just won't do that to myself again. I'll talk with you about everything and anything I want to or I just won't talk at all! I'll leave the gap there this time.

Don: It's got to include everything.

Sue: I don't know who I'm madder at—you for doing it or me for letting you. You got your way!

Don: You're mad at both of us, for sure!

Sue: Just mad enough to make sure it never happens again. I won't let it. We're gonna fight this one out. No backing off.

Don: You're firm on that one.

Sue: Don, I want you to change! I want you to deal with what's important to me.

Don: You are plainly telling me you want me to be different.

Don surely got more than he bargained for! He was, if you will, baptized in fire. As much as Sue tried to keep within the fences they had built, she just could not do it and walls were burst open. With some real difficulty, Don did his best to stay with Sue even though the intense anger was coming directly at him. Though unpleasant for both, I think we have witnessed an important and positive breakthrough between them. So much at the moment feels up in the air for them.

But, let's go back and trace their steps, reviewing the areas of her garden through which Sue led Don. She began quite appropriately with clarifying their agreement, what they would and would not talk about. She started to tell what she had been going through, but found it necessary to take a detour to share that her feelings were no longer fresh and she had put them aside. She later moved to being an objective reporter of her experiences—worried, not concentrating, sad, lost, confused, and lonely. We see three noticeable shifts thus far, from clarifying the agreement, to sharing her numbness, to objectively describing the variety of her feelings. The radical shift came next. Sue began feeling so strongly in that moment about that which she had been harboring for so long that it could no longer be contained. The present moment felt so much like so many with Don in the past in which she had been left utterly frustrated, that she could not continue as the objective reporter, but rather cried out her intense rage.

Don did his best to retain his composure and continue listening. Truly, it was an acid test and he did well, after an initial urge to run. Don listened to the negatives showering him. Though difficult for him, he offered Sue a tremendous gift. While it surely sounds like Don deserved every ounce of rage he got, still he kept listening to that which he absolutely did not want to hear.

There was pay dirt. Sue was able to lift a horrible burden that had been weighing her down for so long. Don was able to accept and reflect her thoughts and especially her strong feelings. Don gained some new information that he did not know before. Sue moved into a position of expressing her anger toward herself as well as Don and concluded with a strong request of him.

We have spoken of a process that listening encourages and here is that type of moment facilitated by being heard. Again, Sue did not continue indefinitely: "I hate you," "I hate you," "I hate you." She went beyond that intensity edging slightly toward a need for Don to change.

Remember that we listen for people, circumstances, and feelings. Sue's speaking surely was filled with feeling. The people are easy to identify: Don! The circumstances center on times between them when they had decisions to make or problems to solve. This conversation, as compared to many others, was quite focused upon one arena: Don and his style of not dealing with Sue.

There is little doubt that Don would have preferred to walk in a different area of Sue's garden, but the choice was not his. His choice was to "batten down the hatches" and follow. No doubt he would have rather gone for another cup of coffee, or better still, begun mowing the lawn. His commitment bid him to stay.

A nutshell summary of this form of listening is to *listen to the negative even when you don't want to.* Listening calls for a commitment to an unconditional acceptance rather than the conditional "I'll be with you as long as you're nice to me." While often we are nice, we are not nice all the time. It is when we are not nice that we are in dire need of grace.

Now that we have the experience of one dialogue under our belts, let's go on to another to apply what we have learned. You can imagine that Don was pleased that his men's Bible study group met only a few days following his encounter with Sue. He needed it. He was only too glad to share now the disturbing words he had heard from Sue.

We will be church mice in the corner, for the meeting is held in the fireplace room off the santuary. The men have just finished their light breakfast and are preparing to begin their program. Several men friends will now be challenged to walk in Don's garden.

Don: Am I ever glad to see you all today. I'm in deep trouble.

Luis: Sorry to hear it. Sounds like you need to talk.

Phil: I can see that you don't look like your usual self.

Al: So, what's happening?

Don: Well, you know I talked with John a while back about Sue. Seemed the best thing was to sit down and listen to her. Actually I think it made things worse rather than better. She's really mad at me.

Bill: You must be really disappointed.

Don: Plus lots of other things, too...like hurt. She thinks I'm controlling her in a nice way just to get my way.

John: Like you're putting one over on her all the time.

Don: Sounds like I'm an ogre. She says I'm deliberately being quiet and backing off so she will give in and forget about what she wanted in the first place.

Al: You're feeling badly misunderstood.

Phil: Like you're falsely accused.

Don: That's right. I just don't believe I've been sitting back and saying, "Okay, Sue, now watch me get you this time." But she thinks I have.

Luis: You two sure have different opinions about this.

Don: True. I do withdraw. I do get quiet. But I just have never thought I did it to get my way. I just don't think I've been that mean...or even thought much about why I do it. Funny...maybe she knows me better than I do.

John: You at least agree that you don't talk, but not about why.

Don: Agreed. That's where I need your help. It's got me all confused now. Which one of us is seeing it right? I can't just say she's wrong, but I'm not totally out in left field either.

Bill: You do really need to know what's true.

Don: Yes. And part of what's true is that I think a lot about Sue when I make decisions, wondering what's best for her. I really don't leave her out. I guess it kind of burns me to think she doesn't know that.

Phil: You do keep Sue in mind when you're making decisions.

Don: Yes....Well, it bugs me. I thought it was my duty, part of my job, to make decisions. I do that job. I do take her interests to heart. I just don't go off half-cocked, willy-nilly, doing what I want. Then she slams me for doing my job.

Al: You're upset because you can't win with her.

Don: I even ask her opinions on the big ones. She doesn't seem to know how much she does affect me. Lots of times I sacrifice for her and the kids and she doesn't even know it. I do things to make it better for all of them.

Luis: She's in on your big decisions.

Don: I suppose it's the same way with you all. I love her and I want her to be happy. But I don't seem to be given credit for that.

John: You do love her.

Bill: Sounds like you hurt when Sue doesn't recognize it.

Don: I've given her a lot. I've provided a lot. When we came back here she had a ready-made family, friends, a good home. We didn't have to go through the usual struggle of finding all that. My folks were good to her and my friends took a liking to her right away.

Phil: You offered her a whole circle of people.

Don: And I know that helped her. She fit right in and we moved along faster with our lives than most. I helped her with the kids, too. Took them places and went to all their games and school programs. I even made time for the two of us, so we weren't always caught up in family things.

Al: You have done a lot for Sue.

Don: I have. And what really bothers me is that she makes so much out of one weak spot. So I get quiet and back off. Why doesn't she look at all the good things I'm doing instead of making a big deal out of that flaw in me?

Bill: You're angry about that!

Luis: Sounds like you feel misunderstood, too.

Don: You're right. Seems like I go in circles. I go from being angry to being hurt to feeling sorry for myself. Swirling around is no fun. I've got to get a direction.

John: You can't stay there, going from one feeling to another.

Don: But I didn't come here this morning just to complain or to have you tell me how right I am and how wrong Sue is. That seems unfair. After all, she isn't here to tell her side of it....There's no doubt, she sees something wrong in me. I can't get away from that fact. Would I really do what she's saying I'm doing?

Bill: That's the real question you're facing.

Don: In a way it's hard to talk about. You know how something is hard to admit...like a kid caught with his hand in the cookie jar. It's embarrassing, I guess.

Phil: It's not easy to look at the idea that you might just be doing what Sue says you are.

Don: Right. I'd hate to think that I was intentionally doing something against her. Do I really set out to make her a nobody by getting my way? Guess I'd better do a little looking back at how things have gone.

Al: So, you really need to check that out.

Luis: Sounds like a good thing to do.

Don: But it's hard. Now I've got to size myself up in a new way. Through Sue's eyes. All right...so coming back to Wenatchee was probably our first big decision. I really thought that she was excited and ready...but then I don't remember that we had a formal sit-down talk about it.

John: You thought Sue was excited, even if you hadn't talked much.

Don: That's true. And then there was that brick house near her school that she really liked when we were ready to leave the apartment and buy. We looked at it once, but she didn't say much about it after my folks offered us an acre of their orchard property to build on.

Phil: You don't remember hearing much from Sue on that.

Don: Well...she said several times how she worried about being that close to the folks, but I didn't think that she was really serious. She didn't seem to object when I set a time to see the architect about plans.

Al: You didn't hear strong feelings from her.

Don: I guess I heard more about the orchard. She really did not want to take that on. She thought all our spare time would go there, weekends and such. I know she talked about needing times to go to Seattle so the kids would have a chance to be with their other grandparents. Come to think of it, she said it was unfair that we lived right by my parents, but didn't get to see her parents very often. I guess I had forgotten that.

Bill: Sue did really speak out against the orchard.

Don: Yes...she really did. I played it down. I guess I wanted that orchard so badly that I didn't want to hear her. I ended up not talking about it...just went ahead. We leased it from the folks.

John: So to get what you wanted you had to close Sue out.

Don: I guess....I suppose I never heard her speak as strongly as she did. I softened it...or heard what

I wanted to. Gosh, that's hard to admit....It must mean Sue is right. But, wait....No, it wasn't on purpose. I didn't do it against her.

Luis: You did it for you, but not against her.

Don: Do you know what it's like? It's like an alarm goes off inside my head. It's so familiar to me. It's like a danger signal. Something says I'm getting too close and its scary.

Al: You mean, like your automatic pilot takes over.

Don: I think so. Well—here—it's like if I really said to myself that Sue point-blank doesn't want the orchard, then the signal goes off. I guess...well...I wouldn't know what to do.

Phil: Like you're confused.

Don: That's it. I get lost, all fogged up. The message comes loud and clear. Back off! Get away! Mayday! Mayday! You are in clear and imminent danger!

Bill: Those are strong "get-away" feelings!

Don: Yes. It's like there's a fight ahead. There's no way to avoid it and I've got to.

Luis: It's urgent. You've got to avoid a fight at all costs!

Don: Sure...that's what's been going on! I will not fight! I simply will not fight with Sue. Not just with Sue, with anybody. I just won't fight. I couldn't count the number of times I've said to Sue that I'm not a fighter. Fighting doesn't get you anything.

John: You are totally convinced of that.

Don: It's for my own sake. It's something I have to keep away from. I have to keep myself out of that. It's different than wanting to control Sue. It feels different.

Phil: So you're keeping yourself out of trouble.

Don: Oh, wow! That word *trouble* seems to strike a chord. It really smarts....

Don's sharing is understandably not as feeling-filled as was Sue's. His friends follow as Don shifts from one focus to another: relief at being with them, being in trouble with Sue, feeling badly misunderstood by her, confusion about who is right, defending his way of making decisions, justifying all that he has given Sue, and anger that Sue magnifies one supposedly small flaw.

A major shift occurs when Don, after justifying himself at length, wonders if he would really do what Sue says he does. Then, Don reviews how he may, in fact, have closed Sue out of decisions, but he vehemently denies any motive to get his way. Finally, Don shifts into the strong "get-away" feeling that comes over him whenever a conflict might be in the offing.

Don walked his friends through those areas of his own garden. They did a nice job of allowing him to lead on, especially in not confronting his need to justify and defend himself. They may have known, or at least sensed, that Don would come back later to deal with Sue's concern. He did. Accepting his justifications probably helped him to look at how he had been making major decisions. To have jumped in and critized Don would have hardened his argument.

Neither did they jump on the bandwagon and agree fully with Don that Sue was surely uncaring not to appreciate all that Don had done for her. Either to criticize or rush in to defend Don would not be walking in his garden. Following him in his own moving process is the adventure.

Don comes finally to a rather intriguing and disturbing sense of "trouble" whenever conflict dawns on the horizon. Where this newly sensed feeling will lead Don, no one as yet can tell. There is only the sense that this sharing has left him in a different place than he began. The bubbling, moving, churning process within Don is at work.

I claim that God, the *abba-imma* of Jesus, was involved in these two sharing events. I believe this to be true because my faith tells me that God is intimately present in each and every moment of our lives. But more specifically, I think that God was involved in some special ways because of the listening that was occurring. Listening offered God some opportunities that were not usually present in the ordinary daily events of Don and Sue. Listening helped to set the stage for some new happenings. Listeners were in a sense cooperating with God's desires for these two persons, helping those desires to be fulfilled.

The claim I have made needs elaboration. I affirm that God draws us toward greater honesty, authenticity, and genuineness. Such is God's desire for us. God lures us continually in that direction. We many times do not follow that lure; often the conditions just don't seem ripe to do so. We go for the usual, rather than the new. Sue had harbored unfair and unjust feelings for some time and seemed to be able to bury them, set them aside, and avoid them.

Then Sue and Don set the stage. Touching so close to this area of hurt, Sue's lure by God to be genuine met with Don's new decision to be present to her. Intensity resulted! That which had been hidden, burst forth. Injustice and unfairness came forth crying for righteousness! In Sue's garden there was an area that had been overgrown and hidden by thick underbrush. An opening was made. The hidden was revealed.

God was luring both: Sue toward authenticity, Don toward presence. That moment, following upon thousands of other moments of luring, became the one in which the conditions were friendly and it happened. God was present with each in their speaking and listening, persuading their shaping and forming of each word and feeling.

Still, God was not any more or any less present than in every situation of Sue's past, feeling with her what she felt and luring her to the next step. The time, however, was not ripe as it was in this moment, in which the creative processes of both blended in a new way. The openness and receptivity of listening to all of Sue, not just to the beautiful, was a critical factor.

If God was luring Sue toward authenticity, then the call to Don appears to be toward complexity. The need was to search beyond his usual beliefs that form his self-esteem. Don would remain in his well-established position, defending himself well, at his own jeopardy. He was vulnerable. With those who caringly listened, Don found the setting where he might expand his awareness even though he bumped headlong into contradictions and embarrassments.

I affirm that the one who is complex calls us to ever-increasing complexity. Better that we have strange bedfellows in our psyche than that we be boringly narrow. Indeed God, who relates to every entity in our wondrously varied creation, must love diversity. Surely this same God knows and accepts such diversity within us.

So Don too had a part of his garden that was hidden to him. For Don we might see it as a fenced-in area, rather than the undergrowth of Sue's garden. But God does not rip down fencing. That is left to the person. Those men who were willing patiently to hear all of Don's justifications, also allowed him to move increasingly closer to that fence. The ashamed feeling that Don reported and his question about whether Sue might be right about him are clues that Don was inching closer to that hidden area.

Again, I am assured that God had called Don many times to see the fenced area and to begin to dismantle it. Those who listened cooperated with God's deeper desires for Don: that he be complex, whole, authentic, not limited. The fence is not down; only a board is loose. That was enough for this day. The process will continue with two clues bubbling within Don, the alarm signals in his head and the mysterious sense of trouble. After all, our processes most frequently move slowly with tiny steps rather than flashing bursts of revelation. Don will search and, with the right conditions, hopefully find.

So we conclude this form of listening. How strange it is to know how utterly simple it is to describe and yet to realize what a deep mystery it veils. To walk in others' gardens we are called to follow and allow them to show us what they will.

There is wondrous power released when we listen with acceptance to all of the complexities, contradictions, and unattractiveness of the other person. We have the opportunity to offer such a gift. From the other side, imagine being your total self in the presence of another and experiencing acceptance. This spells grace. Listening becomes a ministry of grace.

Now, on to the past!

4

Seeing in a New Light

Then Jesus said, "Father, forgive
them; for they do not know what
they are doing."

Then Jesus, crying with a loud voice,
said, "Father, into your hands I
commend my spirit."

Luke 23:34, 46

To our human eyes the hills around our valley seem continually to change. Only their basic outline can be seen in the "dawn's early light." Yet as the morning unfolds, the contours of the lower slopes appear and the ravines with their sage and occasional evergreen come forth. The afternoon sun reveals even different draws and gulleys as the shadows steal across the face of the hills.

Winter months border the hills with gray, and when snow graces them the distinction between earth and sky is hardly visible. The winter tilt of the earth causes the morning sun to greet us from the southern canyon wall bordering the Columbia River, casting unfamiliar shadows on our hillsides. When clear blue skies surround the snow-laden hills, they sparkle and glisten in beauteous contrast.

On late summer nights the dark blue sky persuades the westerly hills to become jet black, marking the skyline wondrously with a dancing light-blue border. The full moon on a cloudless night gives a "clarity of midday" to the hills, while the brightness of the red setting sun blots out all details of the hills except that which gradually engulfs the glowing sinking sphere. Still the hills remain largely unchanged. We who inhabit this valley are seeing them constantly in a new light.

We may also see our own pasts in a new light. Thus I chose this imagery to illustrate the next form of listening. Not that our pasts change; they do not. Yet, like the hills, we change the way we interpret our past. It would be like taking a picture of ourselves with family, friends, or favorite pet. That picture is set, over, complete, unchanging—except as the photo might fade over the decades ahead. That completed moment is finished. But the interpretations, meanings, and feelings attached to that picture may constantly undergo change. To these we should listen carefully, and it is to this task that we now turn.

We are now preparing to listen to the past of other persons. They will be speaking in the past tense about some event that has happened in their history. The goal is to allow and encourage persons slowly to review what happened, then to put into words the meanings of that happening. Their meanings include at least how they felt, what they decided, and what they concluded about themselves, and are usually found to be interwoven with a part of the description of the event itself.

Meanings are not separate and distinct from the description of the event. The most usual experience for all of us is to have feelings, thinking, values, and action rolled up in one ball together. It is only as we analyze and dissect that they become separate parts. In our natural state they are integrated.

The skills employed here are the ones already described earlier. We reflect and wait with caring. We follow and accept. The key feature of this form of listening is knowing where we are and what might happen. That is, we are reviewing the past with the other persons and we have hope that they may see it in a new light. Here we need to be patient and unhurried.

Our hope is that persons may come to a new understanding of what they did and who they were in that moment, especially if they drew limiting and harmful conclusions about themselves. We listen to encourage persons to see more accurately what did happen, so that they might come to more respecting and affirming beliefs about themselves.

It seems best to take these general ideas and let them be real and specific by once again entering the lives of Don and Sue. Each of them will explore a signficant past event in pursuit of understanding. They are in trouble with one another and deeply in need of this understanding.

We begin with Sue, recalling that she became very angry with Don, confronting him with her long-held distress over his getting his way by avoiding any conflict between them. But she was angry with herself as well. She allowed Don to back off; she dared not confront his retreating. Why she allowed this all these years is the burning question for her as she begins her conversation with a close friend, Jan, who teaches the primary class at their church.

We will be nearby listening in as Sue recounts some earlier events. She desperately needs to find an answer so that she can like and respect herself again. We will be eager to know how Jan helps her friend to see her past in a new light.

Sue: I got so mad at Don, but now I see it's not all his fault. He's done his part, to be sure, but I could have called him on it and didn't.

Jan: So you're thinking that you had your part in it, too.

Sue: I've been turning it over in my mind. Ha!…Just listen to me. That's like saying I have some control over it. The truth is it won't let go of me. I've got to get some answers for myself so I can have some peace.

Jan: You sound like you're in turmoil about it now.

Sue: I see now that it was so simple. If Don was quiet, I figured that he didn't agree with me and I had better begin guessing what he wanted. I worked hard to try to figure that out, and simply let what I wanted fade away.

Jan: At least, it's good that you see it so clearly.

Sue: You're right, it is good. But what I don't see is why that was so strong in me. It's why! Why didn't I just speak my mind with Don when he backed off? The sad thing is that I never even thought of doing that. That is really tragic. Now, I can't believe how much I trapped myself.

Jan: You feel compelled to find out why.

Sue: I've wondered when all of this got started. Have I always been this way with Don? Sometimes it seems like it. When I rack my brain, searching and looking, I seem always to end up back at those job interviews at college. Maybe because after making all the wedding plans, that was our first big decision together.

Jan: So, maybe the interviews were the start.

Sue: I remember that I was talking with reps from several school districts and Don was talking with the apple people. Yes, that's it. It was over dinner that night when Don said that you can teach anywhere, but not many places grow apples.

Jan: Your talk that day seems important.

Sue: Yes, what Don said was really important. At the time it made sense. It was like if I were a nurse, most any town has a doctor's office, or if I were a bookkeeper even the smallest town has a business. It was logical.

Jan: That's true. What Don said seemed to make sense.

Sue: But in another way it doesn't. So, am I second best? Was I brainwashed about being a woman? Is he more important than me? I just bought into it without even batting an eye...like it was simply natural.

Jan: Looking back now you feel tricked.

Sue: That I do, for sure. It fries me the way I got led down the primrose path—wait a minute—the way I led myself. Where were my brains? But I don't remember any struggle in myself. It really did seem like it was already the way things were...simply natural.

Jan: You sound surprised that it seemed so natural then.

Sue: I guess our ways with each other were already in place and rolling right along. What Don said was not just logical, it fit with the way things were operating. The interviews weren't the beginning of all this.

Jan: So it didn't seem to start there after all.

Sue: Of course! How could I forget it...the wedding! That's where it all got started!

Jan: Hmmm...at the wedding!

Sue: Get this, Jan. Picture a beautiful Christmas wedding in my home church in Seattle. You know, with all those childhood memories filling the sanctuary. I can just see us at the altar....I can hear Susan singing the Lord's Prayer just before we exchanged rings.

Jan: Yes. I can imagine that lovely scene.

Sue: And in the midst of that I am whispering a vow to God—but hold on—there's something before that.

Jan: Oh, you've remembered something important!

Sue: That's right! I have...I have! I can see it now. No,
I can hear it now. It was at the rehearsal dinner
the night before. We were all together at the
restaurant, talking, laughing, and giving out
gifts. My grandmother, Dad's mom, was sitting
across from me. She was such a dear. My grandparents had just celebrated their fiftieth the year
before. I respected them both so much.

Jan: They were special to you.

Sue: Yes. During a lull in the conversation, she bent
close to me and said she would offer me some
wisdom about marraige. Well, I ask you, who
would have more right to offer it than she did? I
listened. She told some stories about their wedding, then said she had always lived by this
principle: "My needs will be fulfilled by meeting
his needs."

Jan: So, she told you that your needs would be fulfilled
by meeting Don's.

Sue: That's exactly what I heard. There is where my
happiness was to be found. It seemed so right,
coming from this lovely, wise saint. I believed
her.

Jan: Hmmm...sure! Her principle became yours.

Sue: I believed it so much that when I stood at the altar
during the solo...I vowed...I whispered a promise
to God to fulfill Don's needs, asking that mine
would be fulfilled too.

Jan: What a powerful vow!

Sue: That was it! That's where it started. No wonder it
seemed so natural later. I don't take my vows to
God lightly. I don't like what I did...but it's a
relief to find it.

Jan: Yes, what a relief to remember that promise.

Sue: Funny...the vow must have been lost in all the
excitement of those days...but it seemed to do its

work in me anyway. I tried hard to meet Don's needs and forgot why I was doing it. I cooperated and deferred and made things easy for him. It became like a habit, a second nature to me.

Jan: You certainly gave it your all without knowing why.

Sue: I didn't know why. I put my wants and desires on the back burner and Don let me do it. Why not? He didn't even know that I was doing it.

Jan: You were putting Don first and it was all invisible to him.

Sue: I sold out! I sold my soul! I'd try even harder. I'd listen, watch, and study Don's expressions to learn what he wanted, and then cooperate. My gosh, I even taught the children to do it. I made him more important than I was. I set myself up to be angry inside and not know why I was feeling that way.

Jan: I can see why you'd be angry.

Sue: Jan, what more does anyone have than their own heart's desires? Isn't that our most precious possession?

Jan: Indeed! Your own questions are saying it's so.

Sue: I did not see what I was doing. I do now. I've got to go back to that altar and take back that vow....I need a new one. Maybe, then, I'll have some peace.

Jan: Yes, Sue, it sounds great!

Sue: OK then, let me try it out on you. My needs are every bit as important as Don's. Yes, our needs are equal. And...yes...I must honor and cherish my own needs...not hide them or push them down.

Jan: You've made that very clear.

Sue: Let's see if I can say it. I vow...to honor and

	cherish my needs...no more or no less than his. There! I think that says it.
Jan:	Nicely said. That's important!
Sue:	Even...mind you...if we have to argue them out. The struggle might be good for us. Get 'em out in the open even if it is upsetting and we don't agree at all. I'm ready to do that. This feels a lot better.
Jan:	Even heading for a disagreement feels better than before.
Sue:	Yes. It has to be better than what didn't work for me. I know a lot of people renew their wedding vows. I guess I did it a little different—revoked one and made a new one.
Jan:	And the new one fits you so much better.
Sue:	Sure does!

Sue found a new freedom by looking back! Jan was an important influence! Not that Jan did the superhuman, but she was willing to be patient and unhurried in a review of Sue's significant past events.

Sue sought the answer in the job interviews at college and found that since her responses were already so natural that they must have been firmly in place by then. She was lured to look back farther and was drawn to the vow at the altar during the wedding, which was surprisingly interrupted by her recollection of her respected grandmother at the rehearsal dinner. There was the pay dirt—the gold. Sue's acceptance of her grandmother's principle was the explanation of her vow and her unthinking actions over the years. Relief and anger resulted.

What she had originally seen as a decision to follow the model of her beloved grandmother was now seen in a new light. The principle, which had left her awareness quickly, was an invitation to negate her own needs. First, Sue saw the past clearly in the old light, then in the new light. She vowed the new! She could fully embrace the new equality of needs and decide to leave the old in her past.

To help in facilitating this freeing event, Jan reflected and waited with caring. She went with Sue to each location in the past where Sue paused. She mirrored the people, circumstances, and feelings found in each. She followed, turning with Sue when she turned, not asking her to go anywhere other than where Sue seemed to be led.

Jan allowed Sue to reinterpret, reframe, reconsider her earlier decision. She was patiently present as Sue slowly formed and spoke her new vow. She affirmed her new feelings of self-respect, replacing the earlier anger toward herself. The particular listening skill that distinguishes this from others is that Jan knew she was walking with Sue in her past.

While Sue was searching her past for the source of her own limitation, Don knew the exact location of his problem. He shares a past event with his Bible study group and they walk through that hurtful and decisive time with him. Once again we will be observing and listening to see how his friends offer him the opportunity for healing that he needs. Don offers the first clue to his friends by telling them he had hurt someone and he was now being haunted by it.

Al: Well, I believe it's Don's turn to share today.

Don: I sure am glad. I've got to get something off my chest. I know it's got a lot to do with what's going on between Sue and me.

Bill: All the more reason for you to talk today.

Luis: Sounds really important to me.

Don: I've never talked about it to anyone. I really hurt someone once, and it's coming home to roost now. I have even been dreaming about it lately. It's been on my mind a lot.

John: You've really been going though a tough time.

Don: I expect all of you would be surprised if I said I used to have quite a temper. Sure doesn't show now. Well, I did. You know the old routine about walking around with a chip on your shoulder? That was me.

Phil: You're right. I would never have known that.

Bill: That's not the levelheaded Don I know.

Don: You don't see it because of this thing that happened. And now as I get into it, I feel ashamed to tell you about it…but, I've got to. It's been festering inside me too long already. And I've got to do something about it to help my marriage.

John: I think that we understand about shame.

Luis: Right!

Don: OK, here goes. I hope I can keep it together while I tell you about it. See…I was a junior here at Wenatchee High School…and I…uh…really liked this girl. Her name was Becky. She lived up on Stemilt. But just my luck, she had been going with the same guy for a long time.

Al: So you liked her but she wasn't available.

Don: Not to date. We talked in class and were friends. Then I heard that she and Fred were arguing all the time and the next thing I knew she was inviting me to go to the sock hop. Some of you probably remember those dances, girls ask guys.

Phil: What a surprise!

John: Yeah, and a pleasant one at that.

Don: Right. You could have knocked me over with a feather! It took me totally off guard. She saw me hesitate and thought maybe I didn't want to go with her, but I told her I was just surprised. When I pulled myself back together, I said yes. Then I asked about Fred and her. She said they had broken off dating and she didn't like him anymore. All right, OK, great...now I would have the chance I never thought I'd have.

Luis: Were you ever excited!

Don: Was I ever! I was walking on cloud nine when I rounded the corner by the parking lot. There stood Fred and his buddy, Ron. Seemed like they appeared out of nowhere. It didn't take long to see that Fred was mad and I was his target. I got a big shot of adrenalin!

Al: Wow! You walked right into a hornet's nest.

Don: I didn't even have a chance to think...just felt scared and caught. Who knows what he called me. It's like it was a blur. He said something like I was messing with his girl and I'd better back off if I knew what was good for me.

Bill: Like you were caught up in a tornado!

Phil: Yeah, sounds like Fred didn't think it was all over with Becky.

Don: I guess I said Becky told me it was over between them and that, anyway, she should know what she wants. I had barely gotten it out of my mouth and he swung at me. Without even thinking I swerved to the side and I caught him with my fist. The next thing I knew, I heard this thud and he was laying with his head against the curb, bleeding. He was out like a light.

Luis: That's really scary.

Al: My blood pressure is going up with yours.

Don: Yeah. It's hard to remember...and hard to talk about even now. I can still see Fred lying there. Ron and I just stood there looking at each other, frozen in our tracks. I felt like tearing out of there, but I kept my wits about me and ran for the office while Ron stayed with him. I blurted out what had happened to the secretary and the principal.

	They called for help. We all went running back with a couple of blankets. Then came the endless wait for the ambulance. I can't tell you how relieved I felt when I heard the siren. Ron and I were both so scared we never said a word.
Phil:	Sounds terrible.
John:	No wonder you were scared to death.
Don:	So, there's part of the story. It sure is hard to say it. Let me kind of compose myself again. Let's see... here comes the part that really hurts. He was in the hospital unconscious for several days. Everyone in school knew the story, probably most of the town too. I was the bad guy. I hung my head. I felt really ashamed. How was I supposed to feel when they gave daily reports on the P.A. system before classes? It kept reminding me of it over and over. I worried that he might not ever regain consciousness and I had damaged him for life. I couldn't stand that.
Bill:	I can feel how awful that was for you.
Al:	There was no getting away from how bad you felt.
Don:	I wonder now how I got through it. I walked around in a haze. It really rubbed salt in the wound when Becky ran to his side. Every spare minute after school she was at the hospital. I couldn't talk with anybody about it. I felt mad at him and sorry for him at the same time. My stomach was in knots from the minute I woke up each morning. What was I supposed to do? I couldn't grab the microphone in the office and shout, "But he picked the fight!"
John:	It was so darned unfair.
Luis:	And no way to justify it to Becky or anybody.
Don:	My folks pleaded with me to talk with them. I wouldn't. The pastor stopped by and offered, but I was quiet. Then I found "Never Again!" "Never!"

"Fighting costs too much," rising up in me and bouncing around.

Phil: You weren't ever going to fight again.

Don: And I haven't. I've stuck by that decision. There was no way that I could go through that again. The only way I could handle it was to block it out and go on. Just forget it ever happened and never do it again. So that's what I did.

Bill: So you've blocked out the fight and stuck by your decision.

John: I can sure see why you did that.

Don: Thanks. Well, some of you know Fred, so you also know that he came out of it OK after several days, but at first he remembered nothing about the fight. Little by little his memory came back. What a relief that was.

Phil: A real relief for both of you.

Don: I guess you would say that all's well that ends well. Not so for me. I've been "walk-away Don" since then. If I began to sniff out any chance of a fight, I'd be out of there. No temper anymore for me. I never threw a punch after that.

Al: Your decision really did stick.

Don: But that's the fly in the ointment. It's not working now for Sue and me. She thinks what I'm doing is manipulating her to get my own way. She thinks I'm controlling her. But I know how fast the red light goes on in my head. Automatically I know there's trouble ahead and I back off. It just happens without my thinking.

Bill: Sue really doesn't understand what's happening inside you.

Don: No, she doesn't. She only knows from her side. On my side I've got to soften up what she says...or not hear it...or say to myself she really doesn't mean

Don: that. I have to avoid a fight with her. Who knows what I might do. I can't risk that with someone I love.

Luis: There's no way you could fight with Sue.

Don: But really I think we could talk things out without a full battle royal. She's not Fred and she hasn't swung at me....You know...I guess I've thrown the baby out with the bathwater.

Al: Maybe you've gone too far.

Bill: Made too strong a vow for your own good.

Don: I think so. It was all so scary I just had to get away from the whole mess. I couldn't think and I sure didn't talk with anyone who could have helped me make sense out of it.

Luis: Your emotions ruled.

John: You just had to get some relief, get away, and you did.

Don: So true. But now it's like I have one arm tied behind me. I can't operate well. It's not just with Sue. All the time I am doing things to keep me away from any kind of conflict. I'm sure that I use more energy fending it off than if I went toe-to-toe with someone. Time and again I beat on myself for not standing up for myself and not speaking out.

Phil: You really get down on yourself for avoiding things.

Don: You'd think I would know better by now. But there are those signals—there's a muddy road ahead. It's time that I grit my teeth and hang in there. If I'm going to make it with Sue, I'll have to. After all, she's not out to get me and I don't think there's much chance that I'm going to throw a fist her way.

Luis: You need to be able to disagree and argue with Sue.

Don: Yes. She uses words. Guess I'd better learn to use
         'em too. I knew how to use my fists, then I started
         using my feet. So I think it's time that I use words.
         If I fight, or when I fight, it's got to be with words!

Bill: So now you're choosing words. Bravo!

Al: I'll add my congratulations to that.

   Don did have much to get off his chest and for the
first time ever he painfully put the past event into words.
No surprise that it was spoken with accepting friends, for
we do not usually share such hurtful, painful, embarrassing moments with just anyone.

   Don shared just one event, as compared with the
several that Sue visited on her way to her own new
conclusion. The people were obviously Becky, Fred, Ron,
and the high school student body. The circumstances
were as familiar as the latest television drama: boy falls
for girl, girl likes someone else, girl surprisingly moves
toward boy, and former lover seeks revenge. From that
point it takes a deeply disturbing turn for the worse for
all concerned, but especially for Don. The powerful feelings he experienced following the fight were enough to
cause anyone to vow never, never, ever to enter into that
arena again: panic, misunderstanding, rejection, shame,
and humiliation. Don was no exception. He vowed!

   Surely his friends felt great compassion for him, especially for his humiliation before the entire student body
and community. There was no justice. Had Don allowed
himself to talk it over with a caring person at the time, he
might have felt relief and not reached such a devastating
decision that would hamper him in all relationships there-
after. But such was not the case. Feelings were held in
and the strong vow did its work.

   His listeners heard Don's vow and, even more, the
effect of the automatic signal of danger that he experienced from the time of the vow. In this manner, they
heard how the past was still significantly affecting Don
in his present actions. Putting it into words allowed Don

to hear it fully and to see what his own vow had done to him.

His present relationship with Sue allowed him to reconsider his vow. Knowing that arguing with her would surely not have the dire effects he had feared before led him to see that his vow went too far. A more moderate decision was in order. He need not use his fists or his feet, but rather his mouth to settle issues with Sue.

As Sue was freed from her hidden decision to negate her own needs in favor of Don's, Don was liberated from his fear of losing control, hurting someone, and facing disaster. There is no guarantee that either of them will never face a crossroads with the old vows again, but they will be more ready to have new options at hand. These options will be much more enhancing and respecting of themselves.

Once again, the friends in the Bible study were not engaged in a stupendous action, but using skills that are available to all of us. They kept reflecting the descriptions of the people, circumstances, and feelings that Don poured out to them. They followed and turned with Don; they patiently accepted each detail of the story as told to them. While they must have hoped for Don to come to some new decision about himself, they did not hurry him in that direction. They knew that the need to get the haunting memory out of his consciousness was pull enough on him.

His friends did not persuade Don to talk more than he had already. They were content to leave the conversation where Don left it. No conversation is ever entirely complete, wrapped, and tied with a ribbon! It was enough for this day, knowing that the process that moves within Don will lure him on, just as it had called him this far. We do not know as yet which haunting thought will push next to be shared.

Obviously, I am already intimating the luring influence of the *abba-imma* of Jesus in the lives of Don and Sue. It is to this subject that I now wish to turn. Let us consider more fully what is meant by our past, then ask what part God may have in our past and our continuing relationship to that past.

As I had shared in the beginning of this discussion, a past event once over is fixed forever. No change may be made in that happening. We have the common phrase, "it's over and done with," which I consider partly true. Nevertheless, we in our culture do have the sense that the past cannot be changed. Things cannot be done over again. The past is over, indeed. Moreover, an event just like this will never occur again. Our events are fully unique.

God was actively involved in each of our past events. God was not absent. Even if the event was fiery like Don's, God was present, persuading in every painful step that he took. God was, likewise, present in the conversation between Sue and her grandmother and at the altar when Sue whispered her vow. There is some assurance and consolation in knowing that our past is not without the divine touch, no matter how distressing particular moments might have been.

Nevertheless, we are constantly revising our interpretations of our past events. The event cannot change, but the interpretations can—and do. Often far beyond our own awareness, we are modifying, reshaping, reframing, and reunderstanding our past. We put new frames and matting around old pictures and they look different. We listened in as Don and Sue did that task. All of our growing understandings, as we continue our living, contribute to the re-imaging of our past. It might be likened to a series of pictures sent back to earth from an ascending rocket, each one giving us a new perspective on that increasingly tiny point where a person stands. The point remains the same, but the context is constantly changing.

We may be actively involved in positively changing our perspective, interpretation, and feeling about our past. And God is present in this process no less than God was present in that moment as it was coming into being. Since God is a persuading presence in each and every one of our moments, then God's creativity is occurring as we begin to see it in a new light as much as when it originally occurred.

I feel certain that God desired that both Sue and Don be released from an imprisoning past. They were in dire need of liberation from past events that have operated—and still do—to limit their fullness and richness of life. I have no doubt that God has called them toward fullness and richness thousands of times since their damaging decisions, yet the conditions at this time were finally right: they had to resolve this impossible situation with one another, they were eager for that freedom, and caring friends were present.

God is present with both speaker and listener, persuading them both toward the new possibilities of speaker-openly-to-share and listener-caringly-to-hear. When these come together, things happen!

My conviction is that God has a deep need for all creation to experience increasing liberation and freedom—and that God calls all creatures in this direction. While we have seen earlier that God lures toward depth and complexity, in searching our past, God's call is toward freedom from anything that has kept us from wholeness. As we have witnessed in the two dialogues, limiting vows and imprisoning decisions violate our future potential. Freedom may be in the form of truth, the truth about an earlier situation and the truth about ourselves as we faced that situation. Scripture tells us that the truth will make us free!

Paradoxically, we can be liberated from that which cannot change. God lures us to accept a completed past and to be liberated through our continuing reinterpretations of that same past. We may be a part of that ministry as we listen so that others may see in a new light!

Having explored the past, let us now venture into the future.

5

Hearing the Becomings

*And Jesus looked upward and said,
"Father, I thank you for having heard
me. I knew that you always hear me,
but I have said this for the sake of
the crowd standing here, so that they
may believe that you sent me."*
John 11:41–42

Consider the apple tree. During the winter months the limbs and branches appear to be stark, lifeless sticks. Barely noticeable at the end of each branch and at intervals along its length are small curved swellings. These buds, too, are dark and dormant.

As the cold, icy days gradually transform into the warmer days of spring, the trees take on a rosy complexion when viewed from a distance and a pale green tint when examined closely. In what seems the twinkling of an eye, the covering of the buds parts slightly, revealing a sliver of darker green. Then in another twinkling, tender leaves burst forth. At the center of each new cluster of leaves, there appear tiny splashes of pink and white, soon to be followed by one large blossom surrounded by several smaller ones. Like stars appearing in the evening sky, splotches of pink and white appear here and there randomly on branch and limb until the formerly drab sticks are transformed into a bouquet of lovely flowers.

The blossoms are in a sense "becomings." They are truly in between the bud and leaf that came before and the Red Delicious apple yet to come. They are new on the scene. One day the stick tree is present, the next day green leaves, followed by pink and white blossoms.

The blossom is truly different from the bud from which it came, and different from what it may become given the right conditions. The blossom is a step in the process that is occurring, and has its own uniqueness. If warm conditions, nurturance, and moisture continue, along with the visit of the pollinating bee, the blossom will give rise to the tiny form of an apple.

The becoming of the blossom has a surprising and awesome quality. Even those of us who live among the orchards and know what is to come are taken back each spring by the breathtaking beauty. Small wonder that each May we are hosts of the Washington State Apple Blossom Festival. The valley adorns itself, like a bride in her full white gown proceeding down the aisle.

Just as the becoming of the blossom occurs to beautify the dormant tree, so we as persons experience new becomings in our daily experiences. Like the apple blossoms, our becomings are different both from what was present before and from what is yet to come. The "new" can and does occur for us—not as often, to be sure, as that which is known and familiar, but still it comes. We have new blossomings. And it is for these that we should especially listen.

The becomings may appear as feelings, ideas, images, or sensings. Often they are difficult to form into words. By their very definition, they are not yet vivid, clear, or crystallized. They may appear, as in the comic strip light bulb, as an "Ah-hah!" or an uninvited thought. They are, however, new to the person experiencing them.

The fourth and final form of listening to be illustrated here is to attend to new becomings in the speech of another. There may be a number of ways to express this attending: pay attention to, be aware of, become sensitive to, watch for, be alerted to, be open for, or notice becomings. It may be said that becomings should be underlined, followed by an exclamation point, placed on the marquee, or written in neon lights.

Becomings are the new in our lives and deserve attention. They were simply not present a day before, an hour before, or a minute before, but now they appear. They are the results of the creative process in which *abba-imma* is luring. In fact, they may never have been present in our lives before or possibly have not appeared in a long time. They are surely new to the particular circumstances in which we find ourselves at this moment.

Becomings may hold great joy and excitement for both speaker and listener, yet may appear first as alien or enemy. Often they emerge as the still small voice. They may be tender and fragile, asking for gentle care. They may be shy and partly hidden, needing an encouraging hand to assist them to come into sight. At times they may tiptoe into view, only to run away until another day when the setting is right.

Persons may be taken by surprise by their own becomings, finding their sound to be strange, funny, or unfamiliar. The utterance is usually, "Did I say that?" "Did those words come from my mouth?"

Becomings are oriented to the future, not to the present or the past. The earlier forms of listening focused first upon the depth that can be found in the present, then the complexity that the present may exhibit, finally followed by the careful review of the past. Now, we are listening to the potential of the future, *possibilities*.

For those few among us who may have really enjoyed grammar in English class, becomings are to be found in the subjunctive mood of the verb. They are the "mights," "coulds," and "woulds," of our vocabulary. The subjunctive mood contrasts with the indicative and imperative—the statement of a fact and the statement of a command. The "ifs" of life are found in the subjunctive mood. All are only possibilities that might occur if the conditions are right, much like the blossom becoming the tiny apple if the growing conditions are right.

For grammarians it might be said that God hovers in the realm between the indicative and the subjunctive moods, between the actual and the possible. The actual is caught up into the weave to play some part in that which is potential, a creation of both *abba-imma* and the person.

In our daily lives there are far more tiny becomings than grandiose ones. They might be missed. Whatever their size or import, however, becomings are significant events for which to listen. All show in some measure the touch of God luring us forward.

Now let us turn back to Don and Sue so that we may listen for becomings in the struggles that they face. First, however, let the stagehand prepare for our hearing. We have come full circle now. Beginning with a bud blossoming into a flower, we have seen the stick limbs transform into the apple blossom.

Spring transforms our valley. With the appearance of blossoms comes the rise in our rivers as the snow melts at the higher elevations. The Methow, Entiat, and Wenatchee rivers flow from the eastern slopes of the Cascade Mountains to fill to brimming the majestic Columbia River that winds its way by our orchards and our communities. The highline canal is once again opened to nourish the many orchards, calling forth walkers and joggers to enjoy the winding contours of its banks.

During this year a dramatic becoming has occurred. Quite by accident, several large arrowheads were found when workers were digging to install an underground irrigation system in an orchard near the airport. These artifacts were identified as Clovis points and dated 11,000 years old. This becoming brings with it an awesome feeling of the presence of the first American families living, hunting, and fishing here in our small community.

Within these happenings, Don and Sue live out their daily lives. We listen in as Sue once again speaks to her sharing group while later Don talks with a friend. We can pay special attention to the form of the becomings that they will share.

Sue's group has gathered.

Sue: It's nice to have a chance to talk when I feel better. Seemed like I was always just telling you my troubles. So let me say I am feeling better now!

Joan: You show it, too!

Gayle: That's great!

Rosa: Well, I want to hear more about the good feelings.

Sue: I want to tell you about them, too. I guess I should start by sharing with you that Don told me about this awful thing that happened to him in high school. I really hurt for him...and of course, you know me, I cried with him. He had bottled it up for thirty years. I don't know how he did it.

Anne: What a relief for both of you.

Pam: It must feel good to put down that burden.

Sue: He's lucky to have a bunch of guys to hear him out. He's lucky to have this church. And I'm lucky, too. I carried a burden just as big as his for almost that long. I just know we both feel lighter.

Rosa: Burdens can get very heavy and weigh us down.

Sue: Indeed...but I want to tell you about these funny feelings I've had lately. I really don't know quite what to make of them yet. And they're really hard to describe, but I know they're there. Something's happening inside.

Anne: So the feelings are hard to name.

Sue: Yes. I wish I could describe them, but I sense them being there...kinda mysterious and foggy.

Pam: You know something new is there.

Sue: I'll put it this way. I feel better even though there are reasons why I shouldn't. Dad's health is still uncertain and I think there's a rough road ahead. We all know that, but I do feel better, almost in spite of that. I just can't deny it.

Joan: Things around you haven't changed, but you have.

Sue: Does that sound weird? No...no...I don't really need you to answer that. I know it's OK. It's just new and strange to me. Well...let me try...maybe it's peace or calm...I'm not in as much turmoil. More satisfied.

Gayle: It might have to do with being more at ease or content.

Sue: Right. Maybe it is more like being content in the midst of trouble...I guess. Like I said, nothing's really settled. There's a lot ahead to face.

Pam: Uh-huh, content in the midst of trouble. Nice!

Sue: Yes, it is nice in a strange sort of way. It's sure a new place for me to be. My, it's hard to find the right words...maybe it has to do with trust. After our talk I do feel a growing trust in Don. Don't get me wrong, we've got a long way to go to figure out what we're going to do.

Anne: So it might be a sense of trust.

Rosa: And...like some trust is growing between you and Don.

Sue: I think so. Still, I'm not totally sure. And you know that there's no way I'm going to back down and be quiet about what I want. Not on your life! That old Sue is gone forever.

Gayle: You're really sure of that.

Joan: It doesn't sound like anyone could talk you out of that.

Sue: No doubt at all! I think, though, that Don will

listen…and that's a big one. Perhaps that's what the trust is about. I trust that Don will listen to me. I say that, then I get a bit antsy about it. Like I'm overstepping what I really know.

Anne: It feels fragile, but your growing trust is that Don will listen.

Sue: That sounds right when I hear you say it. I'll have to live with it a while to see if that's what the feeling is all about.

Gayle: Like it may need the test of time.

Sue: Well, it's so different. All these years he's worked so hard not to hear me. Now I'm trusting he will? Strange as it seems, I think I am. So far it's a great relief to be heard by my own husband after all these years together.

Pam: So, relief is surely one of your good feelings.

Rosa: You're trusting in Don's turnaround.

Sue: It almost scares me to talk about it. What if it's like a dream and I wake up? Guess I feel awfully cautious. Funny, at the same time, I feel it is true, rock-bottom true. So I'm like a butterfly flitting from one to the other.

Joan: So they're both there and they're both real.

Sue: True enough…and I am really surprised that I'm not holding a grudge against him. Like, "you owe me one, buddy—and not one, but hundreds! You put me through a lot." It's just like me to simmer away inside with resentment, but it's not there this time. Believe me, I know that old familiar feeling well enough to know if it were there. It isn't.

Pam: So part of what's new is what isn't there.

Sue: That's right. I know that for sure. No cloudiness or mystery there. I think I had another surprise.

I didn't have an answer when Don asked how he could make it up to me. You'd think I'd have been ready and waiting with all sorts of ways he could make it right with me...earn his way back into my good graces. I said I'd have to think about that. And do you know what has finally kept coming to me as I think about it? Nothing. You don't have to do anything.

Rosa: You were surprised by your own kindness.

Anne: Sue, it sounds graceful to me.

Sue: It sounds strange to me. Like I don't quite believe I said it. Then I get scared again. I think I would scream my lungs out if he ever walked away from me again. I'm sure filled with opposites today— on the one hand this and on the other hand that.

Gayle: Like the old and new struggling.

Joan: Yeah, surprises can leave you reeling.

Sue: Thanks for the reassurance. I know the bubbling inside is good, but it sure leaves me confused too. I have been wondering if this is what forgiveness is like. It's one of those things I've done so many times and probably too glibly. Here it's more like strange feelings growing from inside and the word *forgive* hasn't been on my tongue at all. Maybe it's heart.

Anne: So you might be forgiving...from the heart.

Sue: I really hope so. It feels good and it feels scary at the same time. So much is new and untried. I don't know where we'll get when we start serious talks about Dad and Mom. I do get nervous when I think ahead.

Rosa: Still scared about what might happen in those talks.

Sue: But I do feel the confidence. I barely get that out of my mouth and I feel tense. I'm afraid it would be so easy for Don, and for that matter me, to slip

right back into our old ways. How awful! I couldn't
stand it!

Pam: There's confidence and there's fear.

Sue: Guess, I'd better get used to both of them. But, no
matter, there is something new going on in me. It
is just not the same for me....

The new becoming for Sue took the form of "funny
feelings." From this beginning the group listened with
some care to help to crystallize this fragile newness in
her life. As we would expect in a process, there is movement from one description to another by Sue. She cannot
fully define or describe the feeling, but she is utterly
certain that there is a difference in her now. She experiences a knowing, which cannot be denied. She moves to
consider the qualities of being calm and content. Those
feelings appear to be based upon a newly emerging trust
that Don will listen. The fragility of this new becoming is
clearly expressed in her frightened and cautious stance
about even talking about these inner events. She fears
awakening from a pleasant dream only to face the old
conditions with Don.

An equally important aspect of this becoming is what
is not present. Sue does not feel the grudging and resent-
ing that has been so much a part of her life. She is even
surprised by her response to Don's wondering what he
might do to make it up to her—nothing! She entertains
the possibility that she may be experiencing the offering
of forgiveness at a depth she has not known before. The
undergirding sense and feeling is that of confidence.

Sue's friends helped her to make the becoming real to
her. Feelings become words, which attempt to describe
and capture feeling. Words will allow Sue to reflect upon
as well as feel the new becoming. The group has fostered
for Sue a new dimension of her becoming. All was, of
course, exploratory and tentative. There was no effort to
package the becoming with ribbon and bow, giving it a
finality that it just does not as yet have. The becoming

will change and form into something that is not yet. Friends helped Sue to celebrate and caringly bring into focus the new.

In their next meeting, Sue may report that some new qualities have emerged. Others that were named in this present discussion may have fallen away. The process of newness does not stop with the close of the meeting. Just as we saw earlier, past events are continually being seen in a new light, and even this meeting will surely undergo some new interpretations by Sue. Will the calm grow? Will the trust in Don strengthen? Will any grudge or resentment emerge? Will the sense of forgiving and confidence blossom? Naturally, we know the answers to none of these questions. We all live in a process in which uncertainty is a daily companion—and in which abba-imma is a certainty!

We now focus upon Don. We shall see that his particular becoming took a different form than Sue's. For him there came words.

Don: Well, it's been awhile. And there's been a lot of water under the bridge.

John: I'd like to catch up on what's been happening, Don.

Don: Well, you know that I told Sue about my fight in high school...and as you'd expect, the sky didn't fall in on me. Sure, you knew that all along....The problem is that I didn't know it until I did it.

John: Guess that's why you kept it to yourself all those years.

Don: It's good to have it out in the open! And not just that, but I don't have to be afraid of myself and what I'll do. That's a relief.

John: I'm sure you feel a lot of relief.

Don: Funny, though, what's been happening since then. Have you ever had a thought that just keeps coming to you over and over?

John: Yeah…like an obsession.

Don: Well, how about this one: "Hang in there"? Isn't that a scream? I'm driving to work and it pops into my mind. I'm shaving in the morning, and there it is again. Even when I'm about to drift off to sleep, there it comes—"hang in there."

John: So you can't get away from it.

Don: I began to wonder what's wrong with me. Then, I decided to laugh it off. I told Sue about it and she got a kick out of it, too. Well, then I thought I might as well try to make some sense out of it. I guess that's where I am now.

John: It sounds important for you to find out what it means.

Don: I began to ask myself where I haven't been hanging in there. That seemed to be the right question, because it didn't take long to see that it was with Sue and me.

John: So you found out it has to do with the two of you.

Don: That's right. I suspect it has to do with hanging in with Sue. She's sure been pointing out how I've been running away. Every time one of us might get angry, I left, one way or another. So, do you suppose I've got to hang in there even if anger comes up?

John: You're wondering if that would make sense.

Don: Yes, it reminded me of those posters you see with the cat scrambling to hang onto the ledge with its claws. I'd be just like the cat.

John: Right!

Don: But a guy should be able to do it. I know deep down that I would never hurt Sue the way I did Fred in the parking lot that day. I didn't even set out to hurt him.

John: You wouldn't want to hurt either one of them.

Don: It's those darn alarms and red lights that go off in my head when anger is close by. If only I could find a way to turn them off....I'd even settle for turning them down.

John: They are the warnings you've always had.

Don: I really know they're outdated and don't work for me anymore. They only push me to scramble or block out what Sue is saying. Or for that matter, anybody else I might go toe-to-toe with.

John: You really need to change them.

Don: So, maybe that hanging in there is just like those warning signals...bugging me to do something.

John: They sure might be alike.

Don: The funny thing is that I really can control myself. I'm not going to punch out anyone. I use discipline every day and I know I'm good at it. I just don't fly off the handle at the slightest irritation.

John: Like you really don't need those warnings after all.

Don: No. I can stick around. I can use my head. I'm a good thinker, if I'd ever let myself do it.

John: It's like you've got power, if you'd let yourself use it.

Don: Yes...yes...I really believe that. And you know I would be so much freer if I simply trusted myself to use what I've got.

John: Being free sounds better than where you've been.

Don: And more relaxing. Like I can be myself, not always being on pins and needles wondering if someone's gonna get mad about something. And doing all I can to keep that from happening. Gosh, that's too much work and I'm downright tired of it. Just think, if I used half the energy dealing with an argument that I've used to avoid one, I'd be a real winner.

John: Facing an argument would help.

Don: What I've been saying sounds a bit like hanging in there. So, how do I hang in there with Sue?

John: Sounds like you've asked the right question.

Don: You know, I've been thinking about writing to her. Do you remember that weekend we talked about our marriages and we had to write letters to each other?

John: Now that you mention it, I do.

Don: Wouldn't it crack her up if I wrote to her? I mean, like doing the reverse of what I've always done. Not run, but write! I could hang in there with words!

John: Doing what she least expects. Great!

Don: She tells me that I don't want to listen to what she wants. What if I wrote that I was trying to guess what she wanted to do about her folks? I could write down the things she feels strongly about and what she's thinking about doing for them. I mean, I know it would all be my trying to second-guess her. And I would tell her that's all it is.

John: Doing the opposite is to guess her thinking.

Don: That's right. And I really think that I can.

John: I like your confidence.

Don: OK, then I'd say if she wanted to write back, she could tell me where I was off base and even where I was right on. I wouldn't really be trying to tell her who she is. I know she would bristle at that.

John: You mean she could correct your guesses.

Don: That's it. As I think about it, I know more about her than she realizes...and a whole lot more than I've let on. How in the world can you live with someone for years and not know something about their way of thinking?

John: You're excited about how much you do know about Sue.

Don: I do feel that as we talk. It's like Sue has always liked surprises on her birthday and at Christmas. I'd ask what she wanted and I usually already knew her answer. So I think this is what I would be giving her now.

John: Your guesses about Sue are usually close.

Don: It tickles me...but, I guess that's only the first step. I can't keep back what I want too. That would be selling me short. Maybe that's the second letter. It would come after Sue corrected my first one to her.

John: To be fair to yourself you need to speak your wants too.

Don: But here comes the problem. I can just imagine the alarms and sirens going off. They'll tell me to scramble and run. OK, I'm not going to do that. That's right...the new watchword is "hang in there."

John: There'll be the old watchword and the new watchword.

Don: I really do need to take down my fences...all the have-tos and the gottas. Like I've gotta stay here in Wenatchee or I have to stay on this job or live in this house. I can't start facing up to our differences when I've already got a pocketful of things I will and won't do.

John: So you're needing to look at all options with Sue.

Don: I guess if I'm going to hang in there, I'd better do it all the way. I can't guess her wants and then simply tell her, "Tough luck, none of them are OK with me." We both need to start with a clean slate.

John: You're wanting to be fair with Sue.

Don: I don't know, John. This hanging-in-there business could lead me into a heap of trouble. Actually, it feels right even if it leaves everything up for grabs. Right now, I cannot for the life of me know where we'll end up.

John: It's downright scary and uncertain, but it feels right!

Don: I trust Sue...and I'm starting to trust me. So I guess the ingredients are there. I'd better get busy on that letter....Maybe that will make that nagging thought go away.

John: Trusting each other is the ticket. Good luck on your letter!

The becoming came in simple words to Don, as it usually does for all of us: "Hang in there!" The journey of listening for John was to allow Don to play with those words, trying to make meaning from them. It took little ingenuity to find that they were meant for his relationship with Sue, where he had been doing the opposite. The new words were heard as utter contrast to the old familiar red lights and alarms.

The fresh possibility offered new freedoms; the old held him in bondage. When he explored how he might hang in there, he recalled the letter-writing done in a seminar. Don was amused by the insight that he might just be called to do the opposite of what he had done countless times before. The letter in which he would guess her needs resulted. A second letter expressing his needs followed.

Finally Don addressed the issues most difficult to face with Sue, those wills and won'ts of his own making: I will live here, I won't live there; I will do this, I won't do that. They gave way to a newfound trust in Sue and the goodwill they experienced in their marriage. The stage is now set for authentic dialogue and negotiation.

Sue experienced becoming in the form of a feeling, Don as a thinking. They do come in all sizes and shapes, sometimes rather predictable because of the particular type of personality with which we were gifted. Sometimes, though, they appear in the most unexpected of forms, totally strange. Such is the mystery of this wondrous process in which we live. We may well expect becomings in thoughts, images, feelings, or sensations. I recall that the person who created the "benzene ring," so basic to organic chemistry, saw the figure while dozing in a chair near a blazing fireplace. We just never know.

As listeners we offer a special gift when we attend carefully to the becomings in another's speaking, and when we treat those becomings in a gentle and cherishing way. They are truly fragile and vulnerable, like tiny shoots poking out from the ground. They can be smashed so easily by ridicule, disbelief, or discounting. Becomings are, nevertheless, one of the most precious happenings in our lives. They are the tiny beginnings of who we may be next.

As listeners we need to leave ourselves open as to whether the becomings will move on to become actual in some form of new decision or action. While we may wish to encourage that very result, we are called to leave the transforming to the realm of that person's relationship with God. Our task is more to clarify and crystallize what that newness is and what it may mean. In his or her own time, the person will know what is to be done with this tiny new blossom. We have played a significant cooperating role with God by the gift we have already offered.

And now I wish to be more specific about my assumption of God's part in this process of becoming. There is no area where the *abba-imma* is more clear and evident. God offers us new possibilities of who we may become in each new moment. God is the bringer of possibilities. They are most often out of our awareness, just as is the One who brings them. Some surface into awareness, as has already been noted, in strange and surprising forms.

The possibilities center on beauty, how each of us may be a more beautiful person living in more complete harmony with all of God's creation. The lure is toward beauty. It is immediately obvious that this lure is frequently rejected and denied, but at times and in the most unexpected people and places, beauty emerges.

Measuring sticks, guides, and templates can be created. To whatever degree beauty, harmony, intensity, complexity, and love are present for both the person and the wider ecological community in any fresh becoming, it is to that extent that we may assume God's voice to be present in the event. Truly, not every new idea or feeling that we experience is the pristine call of *abba-imma*. Rather when the personal good and the common good are both exhibited, God's influence is the most noticeable.

With Don, new beauty was evident in his taking the risk to do the new with Sue, doing what she least expected and most wanted. His reconsidering all the old requirements and contemplating the exercise of new freedom display beauty. For Sue, the emerging sense of forgiveness and the absence of the familiar grudge and resentment are truly beautiful. These becomings express beauty even if they are never acted upon, but the beautiful increases if they become actions.

As would seem natural, the new beauty must take into account what was present before. The older and more familiar is the ground from which the beauty emerges. Out of Don's rigid requirements for his life comes the new beauty of freedom. From Sue's former resentment comes the new beauty of forgiveness. One is an outgrowth of the other. Seldom do we have radical conversions or transformations, though we should be open for those forms as well.

So we conclude our visit with Don and Sue in the Wenatchee valley. It will be amply clear that we leave without knowing how it all ended. We do not know if they lived happily ever after or if all their new becomings were for naught. We do know that the stage was set for them to be fully present with one another and to engage as they never had before.

I have offered Don and Sue and their struggle as a flight of my own imagination to illustrate how the four forms of listening may be helpful and healing. By entering the imaginary lives of these two persons we were able to see listening in each minute detail. Principles and theories have to land somewhere and become relevant, specific, and concrete. Theologies must do so as well.

I do wish to continue on this journey, however, by entering a final realm of imagination: imagining a *listening church*.

6

Imagining a Listening Church

*And because you are children, God
has sent the Spirit of his Son into our
hearts, crying, "Abba! Father!"*
Galatians 4:6

*For you did not receive a spirit of
slavery to fall back into fear, but you
have received a spirit of adoption.
When we cry, "Abba! Father!" it is
that very Spirit bearing witness with
our spirit that we are children of
God....*
Romans 8:15–16

The large brass cross is centered in
front of the deep red curtains hanging the full height of
the sanctuary. The pulpit to the right is made of beautiful
birch wood and adorned with intricate carvings. Both the
lectern and the altar centered below the cross match the
design of the pulpit. The carpet flowing from the chancel
area down the few stairs to the main aisle gives an
appearance of red continuity beginning with the curtains
high above.

Large beams of laminated wood invite one's vision
upward where countless stained and varnished timbers
reach to the height of the sanctuary. Brass chandeliers
bearing candle-shaped bulbs hang from above. Arched
stained-glass windows grace each side of the room, with

baptismal font on the left and choir loft and organ on the right. Rows of wooden pews fill the length of the sanctuary.

If by chance we were to open a particular hymnal from the pew rack before us, we would find it to be a memorial to Don's grandparents, for we are in the sanctuary of Don and Sue's church.

Behind the sanctuary we enter the narthex that leads into the parlor. To the left of the parlor is the wing where the church office and the classrooms are located. Leaving the church building one way we come to the parking lot; the other, one of the busy avenues of Wenatchee. Looking back we see the contours of the building, a high sloping roof of tile set upon walls of carefully cut blocks of sandstone.

The cornerstone displays the date of this building, 1952, but does not tell the full story of the many loving hands that constructed it. Don can recall as a boy the many evenings and weekends he spent with his parents and grandparents helping clear the dishes of the hastily prepared evening meal and gathering scraps of wood and throwing them in the pile in the corner. Sitting with his grandmother in church, she would point out the particular group of timbers in the sanctuary that she had stained, sanded, and varnished.

Memories abound for Don, but also for Sue. Their children were baptized in this sanctuary and received their first Bibles there. Sunday after Sunday, Don and Sue watched their children run up the aisle for the children's moment. They could recall the children crowding the chancel area in their white robes and red bows to sing the familiar Christmas carols. They sat proudly as their daughter was awarded one of the coveted scholarships offered by the church for higher education. They could also recall the memorial services for dear friends in their church community. Yes, this was a place of importance, a place of momentous events, a place of sacredness to Don and Sue.

Since the goal of this final chapter is to imagine a listening church, I suggest that it be Don and Sue's.

Doing so allows us to recognize that while they have been the subject of much listening, they have been listening to others as well. The truth that is illustrated thereby is that we need to be heard, we need to listen; we are listened to, we are listeners. We are both. Often, within minutes we may change places with another, becoming first listener, then speaker.

The listening church that I imagine would not be greatly different from the one I already know, or from the one known by Don and Sue. Much would be the same. The difference would be in the spirit that permeates the many things we do. Still, that is a deeply important difference!

Allow me briefly to review the central vision that I have been offering here. There is a divine creative process that moves within all life. It informs and persuades every area of our personal and community life. Though occurring everywhere in the universe, the church uniquely affirms this process and trusts in its luring. The church is a unique institution, and holds a unique treasure, admittedly in earthen vessels. Every Sunday in church we are reminded that *abba-imma*, the God of Jesus, is intimately within our presence.

The church proclaims, the church teaches, and this vision calls the church to listen. Not that the former callings to preach and teach would become any less important or be lost; rather they would be enriched by the additional ministry of listening. God lures, sometimes in whispers, to each of us. These lures are not simply for my welfare or yours, but are always both for us and for the wider community, the common good. Therefore, we should listen to discern where God is calling us both as persons and as a community, toward beauty, wholeness, and love.

I will imagine a listening church by eavesdropping at Don and Sue's church over a period of time, thus illustrating listening in a variety of situations. While it is true that imagining it can be a flight of fantasy, I hope to offer here a possibility that could become a reality.

We begin by listening in on one of the most frequent happenings in church life—the coffee hour.

Don: Hi, Luis. Nice to see you!

Luis: Oh, hi, Don!

Don: I read about Elena. Congratulations!

Luis: Well thanks, she was so excited to get on the dean's list.

Don: I'm sure she was...and I expect you and Rosa are really proud of her.

Luis: You know, we are, especially when she was so scared about going off to college.

Don: That's all the more reason to be excited now.

Luis: She called up as soon as she found out. She's on cloud nine!

Don: Well, bless her heart. We'll drop her a note. Hi, Bill, how are you?...

However brief the encounter, there is a special gift to be offered by entering briefly into the world of another. In this case it meant sharing in another's joy and affirming those feelings. Luis is better having briefly met Don. We can do this for one another and receive back the well-being it brings to us.

On this very same Sunday, however, in another part of the church a different conversation occurs that carries the theme of dissatisfaction and concern. We listen in as the choir members put away their hymnals and hang up their robes. Rhonda lingers a few minutes waiting to talk to Cheryl, the choir director.

Rhonda: Cheryl, do you have a minute?

Cheryl: Sure, I just have to make brunch by noon.

Rhonda: Well...I don't know quite how to say this...but I've been thinking about it for quite a while....

Cheryl: I've noticed something has been bothering you.

Rhonda: Yes…well, it has…but it might seem like a little thing—you know—picky to someone else. I've been struggling with myself about even bringing it up.

Cheryl: Well, it's obviously bothering you. I think we should talk about it.

Rhonda: OK.…So, here goes. I'm just not happy with the anthems we're going to do for the Easter cantata. I guess they just don't say what I believe or want to say.

Cheryl: So, you can't really sing those songs and feel good about them.

Rhonda: That's right. Maybe I should be able to and I sure have swallowed hard and tried my best, but I can't. They're too old-fashioned for me.

Cheryl: You're saying you need something more modern.

Rhonda: Yes. These old words grate on me and get me angry instead of inspiring me.

Cheryl: Like, they make you feel the opposite of how you'd like to feel.

Rhonda: I can take some of it, but I suppose I would like a balance with some new ones. I know they're around. I've heard some on tapes and on public radio.

Cheryl: I understand. You're needing some new with the old.

Rhonda: Yes. I can see that some people in the choir and certainly some in the congregation really enjoy those old songs. I really don't want to take that away from them.

Cheryl: You have a real appreciation for others who have a different style.

Rhonda: Yes. I can accept both kinds.

Cheryl: How about this? Would you look around and try to find some of the music you're talking about and bring it with you to practice next week? I'd like to hear them. I'd be willing to come early or stay late.

Rhonda: Sure, I'd like to do that. Late would be better for me next week. Say, I really appreciate your hearing me out. I feel better already.

Cheryl: Rhonda, you're an important member of our choir and you have so much to offer to us. Thanks for letting me know what's been bothering you. See you later!

A dissatisfaction was heard and became the first step in developing a plan to deal with it. As music has preludes, so listening may be a prelude to solving the original problem.

Listening is no less important in the administration of Don and Sue's church. Let's pick up the extension line and listen in as the church secretary answers a telephone call from one of the church members.

Ardith: Wenatchee Community Church, Mrs. Sales speaking. How may I help you?

Gladys: This is Gladys Arnold over at Terrace Heights.

Ardith: Well, hello, Gladys, how are you? I haven't talked with you in a long time.

Gladys: Well, I'm not too happy at the moment! What in the world is going on at that church over there?

Ardith: You sound upset, Gladys.

Gladys: I expect you would be too if nobody gave a darn about keeping track of the money we old folks keep sending in. It's bad enough not to be able to get there anymore...but when you're not even given credit for what you give that's really bad. I'm about ready to quit giving.

Ardith: My goodness, Gladys, you must not have been given credit for an offering.

Gladys: Correct! And I'm pretty hot around the collar about it, because I sent it in for my favorite cause. Why, you know I've been supporting the children's home over in Everett for years.

Ardith: So...you weren't credited with making a special offering to the children's home.

Gladys: That's the size of it, and I feel out of it enough as it is without being left out again.

Ardith: Of course! You feel neglected, and that makes this mistake hurt all the more.

Gladys: Well, it does hurt. It's no fun to be penned in all the time and not be able to get to church and class.

Ardith: You surely must feel lonely over there.

Gladys: You know as well as anyone else how active I used to be.

Ardith: I certainly do know how active you were, Gladys.

Gladys: Well, this latest thing just rubs salt in the wound.

Ardith: How it must hurt. Gladys, I am writing a note now to have Beth check your financial records today and give you a call back right away. I wonder if it would be all right if I told Pastor Ron and some of your friends in the women's circle about how lonely you feel.

Gladys: Sure, that would be great. I really want to get this straightened out. It's all I've been thinking about lately. And...it's OK...I would appreciate your talking to the others for me. I'm kinda out of touch.

Ardith: I will do both things today.

Gladys: Thanks, Ardy. Hope my spouting off didn't spoil your day. I just gotta do that now and then. Bye.

Ardith: Blessing on you, Gladys.

This short time spent by Ardith was fruitful in several ways, the most important being to soothe the feelings of a longtime member. Gladys needed to be heard doubly because she already felt alone, left out, and neglected. She yearned for a caring voice to speak with her as a total person, not simply to deal coldly and mechanically with the financial error. Truly, Gladys has some rough edges, but patient listening can smooth those edges.

The work areas of this church need listening as much as any other. All churches have volunteers who are dedicated to carrying out the mission of the church as well as overseeing the maintenance of the church community itself. Since these persons are already giving time and energy as they struggle with problems, make difficult decisions, and attempt to plan for the future, they especially need a caring personal touch. Such can listening provide.

We can now sit in on the regular trustee's meeting in which they have invited the education committee to join them. We come in during the midst of the discussion.

Don: I know that we are all getting a bit frustrated and upset about finding a solution here. I feel that, too. If you will allow me, I'd like to try to put into words where we are tonight. I turn to the chairpersons of our two committees. Is that acceptable?

Ralph: I do believe that the trustees are at our wits end in trying to press our point to the education committee.

Ruth: I agree that we are not getting anywhere except becoming more confused and lost in this meeting.

Don: I'll try a summary and ask that you correct me where I'm not accurate. The child-care subcommittee of the education committee feels strongly that the former parsonage at the edge of our property should be refurbished and used for a weekday child-care facility. You have researched the need and know that it would be used by many who cannot afford other care in our community. Many children would benefit from a Christian atmosphere. You see it as an important ministry of our church in this valley. A person is available who has the training to oversee this venture and you know of volunteers who are eager to help. Financially it is possible to break even. Do I hear that right?

Ruth: Yes, those are the basics.

Don: Now, the trustees had studied the parsonage situation and were ready to tear it down to provide more parking for our church. That is still their primary goal. National studies show a church of our size should have a certain number of parking places if the congregation is to attract new persons to the church. We do not have the recommended number of parking sites and the space where the house is would bring us to that number. The committee has also looked carefully at the present need for repairs on the house and the likely cost of maintaining the facility if it were used each weekday. These figures look prohibitive to the trustees. Have I said that accurately, Ralph?

Ralph: Yes, that's a good summary of our position.

Don: Perhaps...we could put our basic differences in these words. The education committee is pointing out the opportunity that we as a church have to minister to an important need in our community...while the trustees are saying...that we need to provide for church growth. They both appear to be significant values, worthy of our attention. Perhaps if we can focus on them, our discussion might be more productive.

Ruth: Thanks for the summary, Don, now maybe we can....

We leave this meeting without the resolution that hopefully will come. The illustration is simply to show that Don, as a trustee, may for a significant moment leave his role and take on the listening role. By fairly and honestly attempting to present both viewpoints, he offers a gift to that gathering that may be the impetus to progress. Again, the task is walking in another's garden by setting aside one's own limited perspective for the common good.

Those who are counted among the saints in any congregation are the church school teachers. Frequently they miss all or most of the worship experience for weeks and face a class of children, some of whom will be present this Sunday and possibly not again for several weeks. They give greatly and deserve most of all to receive the gift of listening.

Today we are standing in the hallway in the classroom wing of the church facility. In fact, we are almost run over by the stampede of children rushing to show their parents their latest work of art. Sue pauses for a moment to speak to a friend, Marty, before leaving. Marty is standing by the window staring out toward the park.

Sue: A penny for your thoughts!

Marty: Oh, Sue, you're just what I need right now.

Sue: Is something wrong, Marty?

Marty: That is without a doubt the understatement of the day.

Sue: You are upset!

Marty: I am at my wit's end with that Brad. I simply do not know if I can face another hour with him here.

Sue: Yes, Brad is a hard one. You've really had it.

Marty: Sue, I have tried everything...everything. I have praised that boy. I have threatened that kid. I have sent him with Megan to get stuff. Just to give me a little relief from his constant bombardment. I have not found anything that works.

Sue: I hear you. You've tried it all and nothing works.

Marty: I am a certificated teacher. I teach kids all week, for six hours a day. You'd think I could handle Brad for just one hour here at church. What am I doing wrong?

Sue: You're one of the best teachers we have here, Marty, but I understand what you're saying.

Marty: I feel like quitting!...But I don't want any fourth grader to think he can drive me away. I've got some pride. And I'm a fighter. In my worst moments I've calculated how I could get Brad to quit.

Sue: Feels like one of you has to go.

Marty: Part of it is that I like the kids, and when Brad isn't there we have a great time together. I like what we're teaching.

Sue: No, you sure don't want one child to spoil it for all of you.

Marty: That is right...right! There's too much at stake to simply let him run roughshod through this church school year after year. He'd be the same with whoever took over from me and the same next year for some poor unsuspecting, glassy-eyed new teacher.

Sue: Yes, he might just learn that he can get away with whatever he wants.

Marty: I will not allow him to do that to me and to the class.

Sue: Good for you!

Marty: And you know me when I get on my high horse. There isn't much that stops me....But what am I gonna do? You know as well as I do that his folks don't know much more than I do how to keep him in line.

Sue: You won't get much help from them. They're baffled, too.

Marty:　And you know, as much as I get bent out of shape with him, I do have a soft spot in my heart for him. He does have his good moments and you see the better part shining through. I can't just give up on him either.

Sue:　Brad does have his good points, too.

Marty:　I have got to have help with this, Sue. I cannot solve it alone. I've tried and it drives me crazy. I really need the help of you other teachers.

Sue:　Sounds like a good idea. We all meet those kids who throw us for a loop.

Marty:　What if I talked with Robin and we set a time to talk about this problem at our teacher's meeting. Maybe the pastor could join us. I need all the ideas I can get.

Sue:　For all of our sakes, it sounds like a great idea. I sure want to help.

It was well that Sue looked in on Marty on this Sunday. She may well have saved the church school a resignation in the mail the next week. Listening is timely, and some situations need to be caught in the spur of the moment before a decision is crystallized that may be radical and harmful. Not that this short conversation resolved the issue with Brad, but it set the stage to do so. Again, in this case, listening served as a prelude for that which will come. Sue offered a wonderful gift, not only to Marty but to the congregation, by helping in an exasperating moment.

If instead of standing in the hallway on this Sunday, we had been seated in a pew during worship, we would have experienced the result of another important form of listening. Entering quietly we may hear the beginning of Pastor Ron's sermon.

This has been a most difficult week for our community. Two young men in the prime of their lives were drowned in a tragic boating accident.

Our high school students and staff have been in mourning. Indeed, so has our entire valley. As I have walked among you these past days, I have heard your sadness, pain, and heartfelt questions. I have heard you struggle about the part of God in this tragedy. In light of what I have heard, I feel compelled to address the profound questions that family, loved ones, friends, and classmates have been raising. Will you, then, join me as I focus our attention on the God of Jesus Christ and the occurrence of tragedy. Let us begin by joining our hearts in prayer....

Clearly the sermon on that day was relevant because the pastor had been quietly and intently listening to the events of the valley. The sermon became a dialogue between questions heard and answers offered. The sermon began with listening.

Within this church of my imagination, listening plays an important role in teaching as well as preaching. We do know that if we are to help persons learn, we must begin with where they are at present. The new must integrate with the already known. Persons learn by struggling to form their opinions and beliefs into words and are influenced by the genuine words of other learners.

Dialogue—speaking and listening—promotes learning. On this same Sunday at church we might sit with one of several adult classes. We enter the class, which on this day is dealing with Christology. The teacher-moderator is speaking.

Ellen: So, Mike has just told us that he believes that Jesus was truly God in his person, while human in his body. He has helped us to see clearly this view of Christology.

Paula: I just can't believe that. I know that it's traditional, but it doesn't make sense to me.

Ellen: Paula sees it some other way than Mike. Say more if you will.

Paula: Well—you know—this is hard to put into words. But I'll try. If Jesus was God, then Jesus didn't really suffer, God did. How can I feel that Jesus suffered and even died for me, when it wasn't him that did it at all?

Ellen: Paula is finding two ideas that don't fit for her: Jesus suffered and died for us...Jesus in person was really God, so God suffered.

Paula: That's right. Hearing you say it back helps me to think more clearly about it.

Mike: Well, maybe the way out of that is to see that God's will was in Jesus and the rest of the person was Jesus.

Ellen: Notice how Mike is making a distinction that may now solve the problem Paula was facing.

Mary: Well, that may take away one problem, but for me it creates another one. If the will within Jesus was not really his own, but God's, then Jesus didn't have any true freedom to choose. It was all God's doing. Like...Jesus didn't really choose the cup of suffering and death.

Ellen: Mary has shown us that the solution has a great problem in it too. If we narrow down the part of Jesus that was fully God into the will, then Mary shows us that Jesus was not free.

Luis: OK, gang, I'm confused. Isn't there any good answer to this Christology issue? Does every solution have a bigger problem in it?

Class: *(Laughter!)*

Ellen: Well...Luis has put his finger on the pulse for us....

And so goes the class: learning by groping, while the moderator clarifies each difficult step of the way. As we have seen so many times before, seldom do sessions end with clear-cut answers. But positions, opinions, viewpoints, and beliefs do gradually form and crystallize. Teaching through the mode of listening in our imaginary church can be exciting and engaging for both moderator and participants.

This imaginary church also has a youth program, where the need for listening is as great or greater than any other phase of the congregational life. Youth are facing serious choices and making important decisions that affect their future. They, too, turn to their peers in moments of need. We eavesdrop now in the youth room.

Heather: I get discouraged when we have a planning meeting and half the people don't show up. Sometimes it doesn't seem worth it.

Chad: I know what you mean.

Latoya: You're right. It happens a lot. We end up wasting a lot of time sitting around waiting for them.

Heather: I'm really wondering if I want to be president anymore. I always end up feeling like I'm failing.

Latoya: You mean you're thinking that it's because of you.

Heather: Nothing I try seems to help much. We get these brainstorms...I get all excited and work hard at it and still the same old group seems to show up for our extravaganza.

Chad: You're really feeling down on yourself.

Heather: Well, who is to blame, anyway? Seems like over at the eastside church, whatever they try goes over great. They end up with a great turnout and have loads of fun. At least that's what Jennifer tells me.

Latoya: You're comparing our little group to their big one.

Chad: Yeah, I know, it's hard not to do that.

Heather: Right! Well, what have they got that we don't? I've tried to figure it out and I can't...except they've got the numbers.

Latoya: They do have lots of people, all right.

Heather: Wish we could get some to transfer over here and give us a lift.

Chad: So you're thinking that more people would make it better for us.

Heather: At least we'd have a few more people to be friends with or date. More choices and variety, I guess. So, it wouldn't matter what you're doing, it would be fun just being together.

Chad: So it comes down to having people you just enjoy being with no matter what.

Latoya: Sure, I can see that.

Heather: Yeah, that's a big part of it. Now, I'm not saying that the program isn't important, just that people are more important. I suppose if I didn't think that, I would have shipped over to the eastside a long time ago. I know I'm just not comfortable with what they believe.

Latoya: Guess it finally has to have both.

Chad: I know that's true for me too.

Heather: Strange…maybe we've been working too hard on program, when it seems like I need the group more than anything.

Chad: Sounds like you might have something there!

Latoya: Yeah, good point!

Heather: Suppose we could each invite in some people we like already and do things to get better acquainted and have fun before we worry much about program?

Latoya: Sounds like a winner to me!

Chad: I'd go for it. What we've been doing doesn't work.

Heather: Well, let's get a list going of people we know....

Chad and Latoya helped Heather to face not only her problem, but one that affected their entire youth group.

Without such a hearing it is possible that Heather might have decided to resign her office and leave the group, a loss to both herself and them. No one tried to talk Heather out of her feelings or the comparison she was making, which allowed her wondering to continue and some new positive possibilities to emerge from her original discouragement and self-blame.

Our final stopping point on our visit to Don and Sue's church will be a meeting of the altar guild as they discuss the decorations for the fast-approaching Advent season.

Anne: I've got this great idea for the chancel area! It's what this workbook calls a Jesse tree. You take this large branch and decorate it with these tiny lights like we use on our Christmas trees.

Pat: I've never heard of that before.

Ron: Neither have I.

Anne: Well, it all goes back to the idea that Jesus is a branch of the stump of Jesse. We remember the roots of Jesus as we go through the Advent season. Here, let me show you a picture of one.

Ron: Not bad. That has some real possibility.

Pat: Interesting, all right.

Anne: I think it is, too. But I must admit I've had a fight in myself about it. Do you know how many years we've had that handmade crèche on the altar during Advent? And do you remember that it's a memorial for Raymond Wallace?

Pat: I see your point.

Ron: That's not easy to overlook.

Anne: So, I'd like to try this new idea, but I surely don't want to hurt the Wallace family or make it an affront to them.

Ron: I can see how you feel. None of us want anyone to get hurt.

Anne: So the problem is whether we can have it both
         ways—a family and congregation that's used to
         one thing and a chance to try out something new.

Pat: I know you want both to happen.

Anne: So far I just haven't been able to put it together.
         I really need your help. Maybe if we each thought
         about it for a week, let the ideas flow, we'd come
         up with a solution....

The altar guild proceeded, using listening once again
as a forerunner to what would happen next. Anne, as the
chairperson, needed most of all a setting where she could
think out loud about a problem that was important to all
of them. As we listened in, she is the one who was stirred
with a new idea for worship. Others facilitated and fostered the bubbling of her ideas.

So we have eavesdropped on the listening occurring
in each room of the church: narthex, classroom, sanctuary, committee room, office, youth room, choir room, and
parlor. The illustrations are simply to show that listening is pervasive and needed everywhere in our church
life. None of those rooms was basically different than
those of most of our churches. Only the spirit may have
been different.

Listening offers something special and deeply needed
by all of us. Persons can come to know that they will not
be silenced, disregarded, discounted, or neglected in any
phase of their church life. Rather, they will have the
enhancing and warming experience of being heard, taken
into account, and cared for. I am deeply convinced that
this experience causes persons to draw near.

This knowing leads me to a connection that is not
usually drawn. Listening may be an important facet of
evangelism, a mission of every church. Though not in the
way in which it is usually thought of or presented, the
invitation to become a part of the church community may
be given by the spirit of listening. People will draw near
to those who sincerely desire to know and understand
them and their life situation.

Although the spirit pervades, this imaginary church looks much like any other. Now I wish to show where it would be different. *This church would have a program to promote listening.* Allow me to place some large brush strokes on the canvas in an effort to begin painting that picture.

I feature three phases of learning a theology of listening: enlivening, practicing, and consulting. The first might encompass six to eight weeks of presenting a new vision with the sole intent of exciting and luring the participants. The goal is to pique one's curiosity and fire one's imagination: listening is a ministry of God in which we cooperate with God's creative activity in the world. This book might well serve as a resource to help reach that goal.

The second is the phase of learning and practicing the particular skills, a more lengthy process. To learn the particulars is to increase confidence and begin to know in one's own experience what listening can do. There is, in my judgment, no substitute for experiencing the joyful results of having listened to another. Resources in the form of skilled listeners and training materials are widely available. What has not been available previously is the theological grounding for listening.

The third phase is that of a group of persons who meet regularly and are intentionally listening in some arena of their lives. Regular consultation with one another is crucial for sharing and celebrating the successes and for struggling together with the difficulties. Building up one another is the keynote, encouraging one another by knowing that even if during any given meeting one person had few noticeable results, others had meaningful experiences.

In this phase, especially, it is important that persons have the freedom to listen to whomever they choose. Probably in many instances it would be within their own extended family, while for others it may be their teaching or work area within the church community or their ca-

reer. Persons are most successful at what they have
chosen to do. If unclear in the beginning, gradually, I
believe, persons can become increasingly aware of where
they are called to listen. This process of awareness is to
be encouraged and enhanced.

I feature the consultative group as continuing indefinitely as a recognized mission of the church. As new
persons complete the earlier phases, they would be invited into consultation. Hopefully, this group could become leaven in the bread of the life of the church.

By these large brush strokes I have attempted to say
again that listening is an every-person ministry, not one
that is specialized and accomplished by a few. I am not
suggesting that only ordained persons be listeners, or
that a particular cadre of laypersons become specialized
to offer counseling in the church or wider community.
Those services already exist in many churches. I am
saying that all of us long for and deeply need to be heard,
and nearly all of us are capable of listening. I desire that
listening become integrated into the repertoire of every
person.

Now it is well that we look at the reason for continuing consultation. Listening carries risks! All adventures
do. Such risks can be recognized in advance and dealt
with by sharing with others engaged in this ministry.
Allow me to consider with you some risks that I have
seen and felt, and then follow them with the joys of
listening.

The basic risk I see is that listening seems a strange
thing to do. It truly sounds funny! It may seem to be
merely "parroting" another person, acting too formal, or
"playing" counselor. It is not what is heard on the television sit-coms or read in the usual novel. It is a strange
language. The risk is in trying it for yourself, diving off
the high board and trusting that it just might be helpful
for you. At first glance it may not seem to be so.

As with most new tasks, the fear is that I will feel
foolish or be embarrassed. Others will surely "make fun"
of me. I will surely fall on my face as I take my first steps.

All of these are dangers and need to be heeded. But there is still a place for risking a mistake and appearing the fool.

Indeed, this entire book is a work of "foolish" imagination, knowing that most of our talk to one another is radically different from what appears on these pages. Only as we imagine may we call into being the new way. So the basic risk is to try something strange and different.

Other risks are lurking in the background, ready to spring forward. We face others who are truly different from ourselves, who embrace different values and styles. We confront those who are angry at us or at what we treasure. We may become warmly attracted and sexually aroused by others and others may feel so with us. We may see no blossoming or growth in the others, but rather a continuing repetition of the same old position.

We may wish dearly to tell others the right answer, the good solution, or the best direction. We may feel strong urges to ask questions of others to satisfy our own curiosity. We may feel deep pain or dread with others and avoid feeling their pain. We may wish to minimize the uncertainty and complexity of others to protect ourselves from those discomforts. We may not agree with the "becomings" that are becoming increasingly powerful in others. We may fear the loss of our own selves as we enter so fully into the lives of others.

I have felt all of those risks. There are no full and complete protections against them. Risks are present. Again, every challenging adventure carries them. In listening, we do enter into the pain and suffering of the world. Yet, the whispering reminder of the *abba-imma* who accompanies us on the adventure is reassuring. Ministy is not without risk.

My experience is that the joy outweighs the risk. The primary joy is the affirmation that we are gift-givers. The reward is in the offering. The gift of listening is given without conditions set upon what is to be done with the gift. We listen, not knowing the response of others to our listening.

We trust that we are cooperating with God's creative grace in the world, persuading who persons will become in the next moment. This joy, I believe, may allow us to develop the discipline and face the risks involved. Eventually there is great joy in experiencing with others their delightful and frightening transformations: tingling sensations, wondrous awe, deep satisfaction!

Finally, God's grace is present with all creation, not simply with human persons. I affirm that it is important that we listen to the wordless, to that which does not speak our language. It is not by mere chance that I have illustrated with images of nature. By doing so I have been proposing that the creation is important, and that if we will but pause and listen, we may hear the longings of the planet and respond with loving care.

I conclude this adventure of imagination into which I have invited you. My benediction is: may God richly bless you as you offer the gift of listening!